POEMS 1956–1973

by Thomas Kinsella

PEPPERCANISTER POEMS 1972–1978

*

THE TAIN

THOMAS KINSELLA

POEMS
1956-1973

WAKE FOREST UNIVERSITY PRESS

Set in Baskerville type
in the Republic of Ireland at
the Dolmen Press
for
Wake Forest University Press
Winston-Salem, North Carolina 27109

Designed by Liam Miller
Cover by Richard Murdoch

*

This edition first published 1979

Library of Congress Catalog No. 79–63668

ISBN 0-916390-08-x *cased*

ISBN 0-916390-11-x *paper*

CONTENTS

NEW POEMS 1973
NOTES FROM THE LAND OF THE DEAD

OTHER POEMS

ACKNOWLEDGEMENTS

Portions of this volume have previously appeared under the following imprints: The Athenaeum Press, Boston, Mass.; The Cuala Press, Dublin, Ireland; The Dolmen Press, Dublin, Ireland; Alfred A. Knopf, N.Y.; and The Pym-Randall Press, Cambridge, Mass.

FOR ELEANOR
WITH LOVE

from
POEMS
1956

NIGHT SONGS

I

Now, before I sleep,
My heart is cut down,
Nothing — poetry nor love —
Achieving.

Turns again in my room,
Alas, the crippled leopard.
Paw-pad, configured
Yellow light of his eyes,
Pass, repass, repass.

Quiet, my hand; he is tame.

Soon, while I lie, will step
And stir the sunken dawn.

II

Before I woke there entered in
A woman with a golden skin
    That tangled with the light.
A tang of orchards climbed the stair
And dwindled in the waxen air,
    Crisping the midnight,
And the white pillows of my bed
On apple-tasted darkness fed.
    Weakened with appetite
Sleep broke like a dish wherein
A woman lay with golden skin.

MIDSUMMER

Hereabouts the signs are good.
Propitious creatures of the wood
    After their fashion
Have pitied and blessed before our eyes.
All unpremeditated lies
    Our scattered passion.

Flowers whose names I do not know
Make happy signals to us. O
    Did ever bees
Stumble on such a quiet before!
The evening is a huge closed door
    And no one sees

How we, absorbed in our own art,
Have locked ourselves inside one heart,
    Grown silent and,
Under beech and sacred larch,
Watched as though it were an arch
    That heart expand.

Something that for this long year
Had hid and halted like a deer
    Turned marvellous,
Parted the tragic grasses, tame,
Lifted its perfect head and came
    To welcome us.

We have, dear reason, of this glade
An endless tabernacle made,
    An origin.
Well for whatever lonely one
Will find this right place to lay down
    His desert in.

SOFT, TO YOUR PLACES

Soft, to your places, animals,
Your legendary duty calls.
    It is, to be
Lucky for my love and me.
    And yet we have seen that all's
A fiction that is heard of love's difficulty.

And what if the simple primrose show
That mighty work went on below
    Before it grew
A moral miracle for us two?
    Since of ourselves we know
Beauty to be an easy thing, this will do.

But O when beauty's brought to pass
Will Time set down his hour-glass
    And rest content,
His hand upon that monument?
    Unless it is so, alas
That the heart's calling is but to go stripped and diffident.

Soft, to your places, love; I kiss
Because it is, because it is.

A LADY OF QUALITY

In hospital where windows meet
With sunlight in a pleasing feat
    Of airy architecture
My love has sweets and grapes to eat,
The air is like a laundered sheet,
    The world's a varnished picture.

Books and flowers at her head
Make living-quarters of her bed
    And give a certain style
To our pillow-chat, the nonsense said
To bless the room from present dread
    Just for a brittle while.

For obvious reasons we ignore
The leaping season out-of-door,
    Light lively as a ferret,
Woodland walks, a crocused shore,
The transcendental birds that soar
    And tumble in high spirit

While under this hygienic ceiling
Where my love lies down for healing
    Tiny terrors grow,
Reflected in a look, revealing
That her care is spent concealing
    What, perhaps, I know:

The ever-present crack in time
Forever sundering the lime-
  Paths and the fragrant fountains,
Photographed last summer, from
The unknown memory we climb
  To find in this year's mountains.

'Ended and done with' never ceases,
Constantly the heart releases
  Wild geese to the past.
Look, how they circle poignant places,
Falling to sorrow's fowling-pieces
  With soft plumage aghast.

We may regret, and must abide.
Grief, the hunter's, fatal stride
  Among the darkening hearts
Has gone too long on either side.
Our trophied love must now divide
  Into its separate parts

And you go down with womankind
Who in her beauty has combined
  And focused human hungers,
With country ladies who could wind
A nation's love-affair with mind
  Around their little fingers,

And I communicate again
Recovered order to my pen
  To find a further answer
As, having looked all night in vain,
A weary prince will sigh and then
  Take a familiar dancer.

Now the window's turning dark
And ragged rooks across the Park
    Mix with the branches; all
The clocks about the building mark
The hour. The random is at work
    On us: two petals fall,

A train lifts up a lonely cry . . .
Our fingertips together lie
    Upon the counterpane.
It will be hard, it seems, and I
Would wish my heart to justify
    What qualities remain.

from
ANOTHER SEPTEMBER
1958

IN THE RINGWOOD

As I roved out impatiently
Good Friday with my bride
To drink in the rivered Ringwood
The draughty season's pride
A fell dismay held suddenly
Our feet on the green hill-side.

The yellow Spring on Vinegar Hill,
The smile of Slaney water,
The wind that swept the Ringwood,
Grew dark with ancient slaughter.
My love cried out and I beheld her
Change to Sorrow's daughter.

'Ravenhair, what rending
Set those red lips a-shriek,
And dealt those locks in black lament
Like blows on your white cheek,
That in your looks outlandishly
Both woe and fury speak?'

As sharp a lance as the fatal heron
There on the sunken tree
Will strike in the stones of the river
Was the gaze she bent on me.
O her robe into her right hand
She gathered grievously.

'Many times the civil lover
Climbed that pleasant place,
Many times despairing
Died in his love's face,
His spittle turned to vinegar,
Blood in his embrace.

Love that is every miracle
Is torn apart and rent.
The human turns awry
The poles of the firmament.
The fish's bright side is pierced
And good again is spent.

Though every stem on Vinegar Hill
And stone on the Slaney's bed
And every leaf in the living Ringwood
Builds till it is dead
Yet heart and hand, accomplished,
Destroy until they dread.

Dread, a grey devourer,
Stalks in the shade of love.
The dark that dogs our feet
Eats what is sickened of.
The End that stalks Beginning
Hurries home its drove.'

I kissed three times her shivering lips.
I drank their naked chill.
I watched the river shining
Where the heron wiped his bill.
I took my love in my icy arms
In the Spring on Ringwood Hill.

ANOTHER SEPTEMBER

Dreams fled away, this country bedroom, raw
With the touch of the dawn, wrapped in a minor peace,
Hears through an open window the garden draw
Long pitch black breaths, lay bare its apple trees,
Ripe pear trees, brambles, windfall-sweetened soil,
Exhale rough sweetness against the starry slates.
Nearer the river sleeps St. John's, all toil
Locked fast inside a dream with iron gates.

Domestic Autumn, like an animal
Long used to handling by those countrymen,
Rubs her kind hide against the bedroom wall
Sensing a fragrant child come back again
— Not this half-tolerated consciousness,
Its own cold season never done,
But that unspeaking daughter, growing less
Familiar where we fell asleep as one.

Wakeful moth-wings blunder near a chair,
Toss their light shell at the glass, and go
To inhabit the living starlight. Stranded hair
Stirs on the still linen. It is as though
The black breathing that billows her sleep, her name,
Drugged under judgment, waned and — bearing daggers
And balances — down the lampless darkness they came,
Moving like women: Justice, Truth, such figures.

CLARENCE MANGAN

Sometimes, childishly watching a beetle, thrush or trout,
Or charting the heroes and animals of night-time, sudden
    unhappinesses
Would bewilder me, strayed in the long void of youth
Where nothing is understood.

Later, locked in a frantic pose, all mankind calling,
I, being anxious, eager to please, shouted my fear
That something was wrong.

Back to a wall, facing tumultuous talking faces,
Once I lost the reason for speech. My heart was taken,
Stretched with terror by only a word a mouth had uttered,
Clipped to a different, faceless destroyer.

Long I waited to know what naked meeting would come
With what was moving behind my eyes and desolating
What I touched.

Over a glass, or caught in lamplight, caught on the edge
Of act, my hand is suddenly stopped and fills with waiting.
Out of the shadows behind my laughter surgical fingers
Come and I am strapped to a table.

Ultimate, pitiless, again I ply the knife.

THE MONK

He tramped in the fading light
Of a late February day
Between hedges stiff with the wind.
Rough folds of his robe swung.
His boots trod stone and clay.
His blown habit crouched
In the wet daylight's decay.
A spade across his shoulder
Slanted into the sky.
Sunk in the cowl his quiet eye.

A sense of scrubbed flesh in the path;
A thought of washing in cold hours
When dreams are scrubbed off
In a chill room, huge flowers,
Night blooms, accidentally plucked,
Each dawn devours;
Of a haggard taste in the mouth
Savouring in death a tide of light,
Harvest in all decay,
Spring in February night.

BAGGOT STREET DESERTA

Lulled, at silence, the spent attack.
The will to work is laid aside.
The breaking-cry, the strain of the rack,
Yield, are at peace. The window is wide
On a crawling arch of stars, and the night
Reacts faintly to the mathematic
Passion of a cello suite
Plotting the quiet of my attic.
A mile away the river toils
Its buttressed fathoms out to sea;
Tucked in the mountains, many miles
Away from its roaring outcome, a shy
Gasp of waters in the gorse
Is sonneting origins. Dreamers' heads
Lie mesmerised in Dublin's beds
Flashing with images, Adam's morse.

A cigarette, the moon, a sigh
Of educated boredom, greet
A curlew's lingering threadbare cry
Of common loss. Compassionate,
I add my call of exile, half-
Buried longing, half-serious
Anger and the rueful laugh.
We fly into our risk, the spurious.

Versing, like an exile, makes
A virtuoso of the heart,
Interpreting the old mistakes
And discords in a work of Art
For the One, a private masterpiece
Of doctored recollections. Truth
Concedes, before the dew, its place

In the spray of dried forgettings Youth
Collected when they were a single
Furious undissected bloom.
A voice clarifies when the tingle
Dies out of the nerves of time:
Endure and let the present punish.
Looking backward, all is lost;
The Past becomes a fairy bog
Alive with fancies, double crossed
By pad of owl and hoot of dog,
Where shaven, serious-minded men
Appear with lucid theses, after
Which they don the mists again
With trackless, cotton-silly laughter;
Secretly a swollen Burke
Assists a decomposing Hare
To cart a body of good work
With midnight mutterings off somewhere;
The goddess who had light for thighs
Grows feet of dung and takes to bed,
Affronting horror-stricken eyes,
The marsh bird that children dread.

I nonetheless inflict, endure,
Tedium, intracordal hurt,
The sting of memory's quick, the drear
Uprooting, burying, prising apart
Of loves a strident adolescent
Spent in doubt and vanity.
All feed a single stream, impassioned
Now with obsessed honesty,
A tugging scruple that can keep
Clear eyes staring down the mile,
The thousand fathoms, into sleep.

Fingers cold against the sill
Feel, below the stress of flight,
The slow implosion of my pulse
In a wrist with poet's cramp, a tight
Beat tapping out endless calls
Into the dark, as the alien
Garrison in my own blood
Keeps constant contact with the main
Mystery, not to be understood.
Out where imagination arches
Chilly points of light transact
The business of the border-marches
Of the Real, and I — a fact
That may be countered or may not —
Find their privacy complete.

My quarter-inch of cigarette
Goes flaring down to Baggot Street.

KING JOHN'S CASTLE

Not an epic, being not loosely architectured,
    But with epic force, setting the head spinning
With the taut flight earthward of its bulk, King John's
    Castle rams fast down the county of Meath.
This in its heavy ruin. New, a brute bright plateau,
    It held speechless under its cold a whole province of Meath.

Now the man-rot of passages and broken window-casements,
    Vertical drops chuting through three storeys of masonry,
Draughty spiral stairways loosening in the depths,
    Are a labyrinth in the medieval dark. Intriguers
Who prowled here once into the waiting arms
    Of their own monster, revisit the blowing dust.

Life, a vestigial chill, sighs along the tunnels
    Through the stone face. The great collapsed rooms, the mind
Of the huge head, are dead. Views open inward
    On empty silence; a chapel-shelf, moss-grown, unreachable.
King John directs at the river a grey stare, who once
    Viewed the land in a spirit of moderation and massacre.

Contemplatives, tiny as mice moving over the green
    Mounds below, might take pleasure in the well
Of quiet there, the dark foundations near at hand.
    Up here where the wind sweeps bleakly, as though in
        remembrance
Against our own tombstones, the brave and great might gather.
    For the rest, this is not their fortress.

THINKING OF MR. D.

A man still light of foot, but ageing, took
An hour to drink his glass, his quiet tongue
Danced to such cheerful slander. Yet his look
Was narrowed to an angry ember the young
Would pity, if they noticed — rage barred in
By age, inflamed by such a little gin . . .
He sipped and swallowed, with a scathing smile,
And tapped a polished toe. His sober nod
Mordantly withheld assent. He fell
Into an abstract wrecking humour. Should
A man 'beat the wall' whose tatters lack
The act of blood? Better to turn his back,
Let new plains open across the dying coal
Time drops before him — bitten by flaming threads,
Paths that he must people from his soul,
By broken dykes and smouldering watersheds,
A planet he must cross to the dark side
There, in a wonder, to bring forth his fire
And dance on scorching leather . . .
                                    When he died
I saw him twice: once as he used retire,
On one last murmured, stabbing little tale,
From the right company, tucking in his scarf,
A barren Dante leaving us for hell;
Then, loping through that image, under wharf-
Lamps that plunged him in and out of light,
A priestlike figure turning, wolfish-slim,
Quickly aside from pain, in a bodily plight,
To note the oiled reflections chime and swim.

MORALITIES

Bronze entrance doors alive with angels' wings
Mellow the Western face — a field of stone
Furrowed with devils. Saints in martyred rings
Halo vast windows, light as thistledown.
The wagon empties and a hooting clown
Skips up the shallow steps: 'Ho! Feast your eyes!'
Flounced, scalloped, stuffed with hay, gay skin and bone,
Faith, Love, Death, Song, creep after him like flies.

FAITH

AN OLD ATHEIST PAUSES BY THE SEA

I choose at random, knowing less and less.
The shambles of the seashore at my feet
Yields a weathered spiral: I confess
— Appalled at how the waves have polished it —
I know that shores are eaten, rocks are split,
Shells ghosted. Something hates unevenness.
The skin turns porcelain, the nerves retreat,
And then the will, and then the consciousness.

INTO THY HANDS

Diver, noting lightly how the board
Gives to the body, now with like intent
I watch the body give to the instant, seeing
In risk a salty joy: let accident
Complete our dreadful journey into being.

Here, possessed of time and flesh at last,
I hurl the Present bodily at the Past:
Outstretched, into the azure chasm he soared.

A PILLAR OF THE COMMUNITY

Descending on Merchants' Alley, Lucifer
Gave jet-black evidence of fatherhood.
A column rose to meet him from the mud;
He perched and turned to metal. Polished, foursquare,
A noble savage stopped in stride, he stood.
Now gingerly our honest deals are done
Under that puckish rump, inscribed: Do good.
Some care and a simple faith will get you on.

LOVE

SISTERS

Grim Deirdre sought the stony fist, her grief
Capped at last by insult. Pierce's bride,
Sybil Ferriter, fluttered like a leaf
And fell in courtly love to stain the tide.
Each for a murdered husband — hanged in silk
Or speared in harness — threw her body wide,
And offered treachery a bloody milk;
Each cast the other's shadow when she died.

A GARDEN ON THE POINT

Now it is Easter and the speckled bean
Breaks open underground, the liquid snail
Winces and waits, trapped on the lawn's light green;
The burdened clothes-line heaves and barks in the gale,
And lost in flowers near the garage wall
Child and mother fumble, tidy, restrain.

And now great ebb tides lift to the light of day
The sea-bed's briny chambers of decay.

INTERLUDE

Love's doubts enrich my words; I stroke them out.
To each felicity, once. He must progress
Who fabricates a path, though all about
Death, Woman, Spring, repeat their first success.

DEATH

GARDEN OF REMEMBRANCE

Tomb and blossom, quiet as a pond,
Sleep in the vault of noon. A yew, unclipped,
Absorbs a thickening laurel and, beyond,
Shadows a thin, obliterated script.

A grovelling bee — the gold drug fiercely gripped —
Lapses half-buried on a poppy's wand.

Into as sweet obscurity have slipped
What honey-seekers of our demi-monde?

DEAD ON ARRIVAL

It smelled our laughter; then, in vivid shroud,
Loomed with averted face (*Dont think, dont think*),
Limped with its poison through the noisy crowd
And chose my glass. It moaned and begged me: 'Drink.'

I woke in mortal terror, every vein
A-flood with my destroyer; then fought free.
I lie in darkness, treasuring in my brain
The full infection, Night's carnality.

SONG

HANDCLASP AT EUSTON

The engine screams and Murphy, isolate
— Chalk-white, comedian — in the smoky glare,
Dwindles among the churns and tenders. Weight,
Person, race, the human, dwindle there.
I bow to the cases cluttering the rack,
Their handles black with sweat of exile. Wales,
Wave and home; I close my eyes. The track
Swerves to a greener world: sea-rock, thigh-scales.

AT THE HEART

Heraldic, hatched in gold, a sacred tree
Stands absorbed, tinkering with the slight
Thrumming of birds, the flicker of energy
Thrown and caught, the blows and burdens of flight.
Roots deepen; disciplines proliferate
And wings more fragile are brought into play.
Timber matures, the game grows nobler, yet
Not one has sped direct as appetite.

FIRE AND ICE

Two creatures face each other, fixed in song,
Satyr and nymph, across the darkening brain.
I dream of reason and the first grows strong,
Drunk as a whirlwind on the sweating grain;
I dream of drunkenness and, freed from strain,
The second murmurs like a fingered gong;
I sink beneath the dream: his words grow sane,
Her pupils glow with pleasure all night long.

THE LAUNDRESS

Her chair drawn to the door,
A basket at her feet,
She sat against the sun
And stitched a linen sheet.
Over harrowed Flanders
August moved the wheat.

Poplars sharing the wind
With Saxony and France
Dreamed at her gate,
Soared in a Summer trance.
A cluck in the cobbled yard:
A shadow changed its stance.

As a fish disturbs the pond
And sinks without a stain
The heels of ripeness fluttered
Under her apron. Then
Her heart grew strained and light
As the shell that shields the grain.

Bluntly through the doorway
She stared at shed and farm,
At yellow fields unstitching
About the hoarded germ,
At land that would spread white
When she had reached her term.

The sower plumps his acre,
Flanders turns to the heat,
The winds of Heaven winnow
And the wheels grind the wheat.
She searched in her basket
And fixed her ruffled sheet.

WEDDING MORNING

Down the church gravel where the bridal car
    Gleams at the gate among the waifs and strays
And women of Milewater, formal wear
    And Fashion's joker hats wink in the breeze.

Past, the hushed progress under sprays of broom
    And choirs of altar lilies, when all eyes
Went brimming with her and the white-lipped groom
    Brought her to kneel beside him. Past, the sighs;

Ahead lies the gaiety of her father's hall
    Thrown open to the chatter of champagne,
The poised photographer, the flying veil,
    The motors crowded on the squandered lawn.

Down the bright gravel stroll the families
    With Blood, the trader, profiting in their peace.

DICK KING

In your ghost, Dick King, in your phantom vowels I read
That death roves our memories igniting
Love. Kind plague, low voice in a stubbled throat,
You haunt with the taint of age and of vanished good,
Fouling my thought with losses.

Clearly now I remember rain on the cobbles,
Ripples in the iron trough, and the horses' dipped
Faces under the Fountain in James's Street,
When I sheltered my nine years against your buttons
And your own dread years were to come;

And your voice, in a pause of softness, named the dead,
Hushed as though the city had died by fire,
Bemused, discovering . . . discovering
A gate to enter temperate ghosthood by;
And I squeezed your fingers till you found again
My hand hidden in yours.

                    I squeeze your fingers:

> Dick King was an upright man.
> Sixty years he trod
> The dull stations underfoot.
> Fifteen he lies with God.
>
> By the salt seaboard he grew up
> But left its rock and rain
> To bring a dying language east
> And dwell in Basin Lane.

By the Southern Railway he increased:
His second soul was born
In the clangour of the iron sheds,
The hush of the late horn.

An invalid he took to wife.
She prayed her life away;
Her whisper filled the whitewashed yard
Until her dying day.

And season in, season out,
He made his wintry bed.
He took the path to the turnstile
Morning and night till he was dead.

He clasped his hands in a Union ward
To hear St. James's bell.
I searched his eyes though I was young,
The last to wish him well.

COVER HER FACE

She has died suddenly, aged twenty-nine years, in Dublin.
Some of her family travel from the country to bring her body
home. Having driven all morning through a storm

I

They dither softly at her bedroom door
In soaking overcoats, and words forsake
Even their comforters. The bass of prayer
Haunts the chilly landing while they take
Their places in a murmur of heartbreak.

Shabby with sudden tears, they know their part,
Mother and brother, resigning all that ends
At these drab walls. For here, with panicked heart,
A virgin broke the seal; who understands
The sheet pulled white and Maura's locked blue hands?

Later her frown will melt, when by degrees
They flinch from grief; a girl they have never seen,
Sunk now in love and horror to her knees,
The black official giving discipline
To shapeless sorrow, these are more their kin,

By grace of breath, than that grave derelict
Whose blood and feature, like a sleepy host,
Agreed a while with theirs. Her body's tact
Swapped child for woman, woman for a ghost,
Until its buried sleep lay uppermost;

And Maura, come to terms at last with pain,
Rests in her ruptured mind, her temples tight,
Patiently weightless as her time burns down.
Soon her few glories will be shut from sight:
Her slightness, the fine metal of her hair spread out,

Her cracked, sweet laugh. Such gossamers as hold
Friends, family — all fortuitous conjunction —
Sever with bitter whispers; with untold
Peace shrivel to their anchors in extinction.
There, newly trembling, others grope for function.

II

Standing by the door, effaced in self,
I cannot deny her death, protest, nor grieve,
Dogged by a scrap of memory: some tossed shelf
Holds, a secret shared, that photograph,
Her arm tucked tiredly into mine; her laugh,

As though she also knew a single day
Would serve to bleed us to a diagram,
Sighs and confides; she waived validity
The night she drank the furnace of the Lamb,
Draining one image of its faint *I am*.

I watch her drift, in doubt whether dead or born
— Not with Ophelia's strewn virginity
But with a pale unmarriage — out of the worn
Bulk of day, under its sightless eye,
And close her dream in hunger. So we die.

49

Monday, without regret, darkens the pane
And sheds on the shaded living, the crystal soul,
A gloomy lustre of the pouring rain.
Nuns have prepared her for the holy soil
And round her bed the faded roses peel

That the fruit of justice may be sown in peace
To them that make peace, and bite its ashen bread.
Mother, brother, when our questions cease
Such peace may come, consenting to the good,
Chaste, biddable, out of all likelihood.

GIRL ON A SWING

My touch has little force:
Her infant body falls.
Her lips lightly purse
With panic and delight
And fly up to kiss
The years' brimming glass;
To drink; to sag sweetly
When I drop from sight.

NAVIGATORS

The swivelled lantern flares, shears
A granite staircase wet from the pier's
Flank and fingers over a strewn
Breakwater in the fog, to drown
Its long beam where the night mows down.

Two shrouded lovers come for whom
Lamps on the concrete sea-wall bloom
And adamant levels under the Head
— Cold contrivances of the dead
Protectors of harbours — spring to the tread.

When these unlink and sigh and sleep
Aphrodite'll walk the deep.
Weaving a garland she will break
A cry from either soul and pluck
The shore-bird's psychotic shriek.

So navigators under threat
Of their extinction overset
The harsh horn and the hollow bell
Against the reef, against the swell,
Ephemeral, perpetual.

A COUNTRY WALK

Sick of the piercing company of women
I swung the gate shut with a furious sigh,
Rammed trembling hands in pockets and drew in
A breath of river air. A rook's wet wing
Cuffed abruptly upward through the drizzle.

On either hand dead trunks in drapes of creeper,
Strangled softly by horse-mushroom, writhed
In vanished passion, broken down like sponge.
I walked their hushed stations, passion dying,
Each slow footfall a drop of peace returning.

I clapped my gloves. Three cattle turned aside
Their fragrant bodies from a corner gate
And down the sucking chaos of a hedge
Churned land to liquid in their dreamy passage.
Briefly through the beaded grass a path
Led to the holy stillness of a well
And there in the smell of water, stone and leaf
I knelt, baring my hand, and scooped and drank,
Shivering, and inch by inch rejoiced:
Ferocity became intensity.

Or so it seemed as with a lighter step
I turned an ivied corner to confront
The littered fields where summer broke and fled.
Below me, right and left, the valley floor
Tilted in a silence full of storms;
A ruined aqueduct in delicate rigor
Clenched cat-backed, rooted to one horizon;

A vast asylum reared its potent calm
Up from the other through the sodden air,
Tall towers ochre where the gutters dripped;
A steeple; the long yielding of a railway turn
Through thorn and willow; a town endured its place . . .

Joining the two slopes, blocking an ancient way
With crumbled barracks, castle and brewery
It took the running river, wrinkling and pouring
Into its blunt embrace. A line of roofs
Fused in veils of rain and steely light
As the dying sun struck it huge glancing blows.
A strand of idle smoke mounted until
An idler current combed it slowly west,
A hook of shadow dividing the still sky . . .
Mated, like a fall of rock, with time,
The place endured its burden: as a froth
Locked in a swirl of turbulence, a shape
That forms and fructifies and dies, a wisp
That hugs the bridge, an omphalos of scraps.

I moved, my glove-backs glistening, over flesh-
And forest-fed earth; till, skirting a marshy field
Where melancholy brambles scored the mud
By the gapped glitter of a speckled ford,
I shuddered with a visual sweet excitement.

Those murmuring shallows made a trampling place
Apt for death-combat, as the tales agree:
There, the day that Christ hung dying, twin
Brothers armed in hate on either side;
The day darkened but they moved to meet
With crossed swords under a dread eclipse
And mingled their bowels at the saga's end.

There the first Normans massacred my fathers,
Then stroked their armoured horses' necks, disposed
In ceremony, sable on green sward.
Twice more the reeds grew red, the stones obscured;
When knot-necked Cromwell and his fervent sword
Despatched a convent shrieking to their Lover,
And when in peasant fear a rebel host,
Through long retreat grown half hysterical
— Methodical, ludicrous — piked in groups of three
Cromwell's puritan brood, their harmless neighbours,
Forked them half living to the sharp water
And melted into the martyred countryside,
Root eaters, strange as badgers. Pulses calmed;
The racked heroic nerved itself for peace;
Then came harsh winters, motionless waterbirds,
And generations that let welcome fail.

Road and river parted. Now my path
Lay gleaming through the greasy dusk, uphill
Into the final turn. A concrete cross
Low in the ditch grew to the memory
Of one who answered latest the phantom hag,
Tireless Rebellion, when with mouth awry
She hammered at the door, disrupting harvest.
There he bled to death, his line of sight
Blocked by the corner-stone, and did not see
His town ablaze with joy, the grinning foe
Driven in heavy lorries from the field;
And he lay cold in the Hill Cemetery
When freedom burned his comrades' itchy palms,
Too much for flesh and blood, and — armed in hate —
Brother met brother in a modern light.
They turned the bloody corner, knelt and killed,

55

Who gather still at Easter round his grave,
Our watchful elders. Deep in his crumbled heart
He takes their soil, and chatting they return
To take their town again, that have exchanged
A trenchcoat playground for a gombeen jungle.

Around the corner, in an open square,
I came upon the sombre monuments
That bear their names: MacDonagh & McBride,
Merchants; Connolly's Commercial Arms . . .
Their windows gave me back my stolid self
In attitudes of staring as I paced
Their otherworldly gloom, reflected light
Playing on lens and raincoat stonily.
I turned away. Down the sloping square
A lamp switched on above the urinal;
Across the silent handball alley, eyes
That never looked on lover measured mine
Over the Christian Brothers' frosted glass
And turned away. Out of the neighbouring shades
A car plunged soundlessly and disappeared
Pitching downward steeply to the bridge.
I too descended. Naked sycamores,
Gathered dripping near the quay, stood still
And dropped from their combining arms a single
Word upon my upturned face. I trod
The river underfoot; the parapet
Above the central arch received my hands.

Under a darkening and clearing heaven
The hastening river streamed in a slate sheen,
Its face a-swarm. Across the swollen water
(Delicate myriads vanishing in a breath)
Faint ripples winked; a thousand currents broke,

Kissing, dismembering, in threads of foam
Or poured intact over the stony bed
Glass-green and chill; their shallow, shifting world
Slid on in troubled union, forging together
Surfaces that gave and swallowed light;
And grimly the flood divided where it swept
An endless debris through the failing dusk
Under the thudding span beneath my feet.

Venit Hesperus;
In green and golden light; bringing sweet trade.
The inert stirred. Heart and tongue were loosed:
'The waters hurtle through the flooded night. . . .'

DOWNSTREAM

Drifting to meet us on the darkening stage
A pattern shivered; whorling in its place
Another held us in a living cage
Then broke to its reordered phase of grace.

*

Again in the mirrored dusk the paddles sank.
  We thrust forward, swaying both as one.
  The ripples widened to the ghostly bank

Where willows, with their shadows half undone,
  Hung to the water, mowing like the blind.
  The current seized our skiff. We let it run

Grazing the reeds, and let the land unwind
  In stealth on either hand. Dark woods: a door
  Opened and shut. The clear sky fell behind,

The channel shrank. Thick slopes from shore to shore
  Lowered a matted arch. I thought of roots
  Crawling full of pike on the river-floor

To cage us in, sensed the furred night-brutes
  Halt in their trails, twitching their tiny brushes.
  What plopped in the reeds and stirred between the shoots?

Then I remembered how among those bushes
  A man one night fell sick and left his shell
  Collapsed, half eaten, like a rotted thrush's

To frighten stumbling children. 'You could tell',
  My co-shadow murmured, 'by the hands
  He died in terror.' And the cold of hell,

A limb-lightness, a terror in the glands,
    Pierced again as when that story first
    Froze my blood: the soil of other lands

Drank lives that summer with a body thirst;
    Nerveless by the European pit
    — Ourselves through seven hundred years accurst —

We saw the barren world obscurely lit
    By tall chimneys flickering in their pall,
    The haunt of swinish man — each day a spit

That, turning, sweated war, each night a fall
    Back to the evil dream where rodents ply,
    Man-rumped, sow-headed, busy with whip and maul

Among nude herds of the damned. It seemed that I,
    Coming to conscience on that lip of dread,
    Still dreamed, impervious to calamity,

Imagining a formal drift of the dead
    Stretched calm as effigies on velvet dust,
    Scattered on starlit slopes with arms outspread

And eyes of silver — when that story thrust
    Pungent horror and an actual mess
    Into my very face, and taste I must.

Then hungry joy and sickening distress
    Fumbled together by the brimming flood,
    And night consumed a hopeless loneliness.

Like mortal jaws, the alleys of the wood
    Fell-to behind us. At its heart, a ghost
    Glimmered briefly with my gift of blood

— Spreadeagled on a rack of leaves, almost
    Remembering. It looked full at the sky,
    Calmly encountering the starry host,

Meeting their silver eyes with silver eye.
    An X of wavering flesh, a skull of light,
    Extinguished in our wake without a sigh.

Then the current shuddered in its flight
    And swerved on pliant muscle; we were sped
    Through sudden peace into a pit of night:

The Mill-Hole, whose rocky fathoms fed
    On moss and pure depth and the cold fin
    Turning in its heart. The river bed

Called to our flesh. Across the watery skin,
    Breathless, our shell trembled. The abyss . . .
    We shipped our oars in dread. Now, deeper in,

Something shifted in sleep, a quiet hiss
    As we slipped by. Adrift . . . A milk-white breast . . .
    A shuffle of wings betrayed with a feathery kiss

A soul of white with darkness for a nest.
    The creature bore the night so tranquilly
    I lifted up my eyes. There without rest

The phantoms of the overhanging sky
　　Occupied their stations and descended;
　　Another moment, to the starlit eye,

The slow, downstreaming dead, it seemed, were blended
　　One with those silver hordes, and briefly shared
　　Their order, glittering. And then impended

A barrier of rock that turned and bared
　　A varied barrenness as toward its base
　　We glided — blotting heaven as it towered —

Searching the darkness for a landing place.

CHRYSALIDES

Our last free summer we mooned about at odd hours
Pedalling slowly through country towns, stopping to eat
Chocolate and fruit, tracing our vagaries on the map.

At night we watched in the barn, to the lurch of melodeon
    music,
The crunching boots of countrymen — huge and weightless
As their shadows — twirling and leaping over the yellow
    concrete.

Sleeping too little or too much, we awoke at noon
And were received with womanly mockery into the kitchen,
Like calves poking our faces in with enormous hunger.

Daily we strapped our saddlebags and went to experience
A tolerance we shall never know again, confusing
For the last time, for example, the licit and the familiar.

Our instincts blurred with change; a strange wakefulness
Sapped our energies and dulled our slow-beating hearts
To the extremes of feeling — insensitive alike

To the unique succession of our youthful midnights,
When by a window ablaze softly with the virgin moon
Dry scones and jugs of milk awaited us in the dark,

Or to lasting horror: a wedding flight of ants
Spawning to its death, a mute perspiration
Glistening like drops of copper in our path.

MIRROR IN FEBRUARY

The day dawns with scent of must and rain,
Of opened soil, dark trees, dry bedroom air.
Under the fading lamp, half dressed — my brain
Idling on some compulsive fantasy —
I towel my shaven lip and stop, and stare,
Riveted by a dark exhausted eye,
A dry downturning mouth.

It seems again that it is time to learn,
In this untiring, crumbling place of growth
To which, for the time being, I return.
Now plainly in the mirror of my soul
I read that I have looked my last on youth
And little more; for they are not made whole
That reach the age of Christ.

Below my window the awakening trees,
Hacked clean for better bearing, stand defaced
Suffering their brute necessities,
And how should the flesh not quail that span for span
Is mutilated more? In slow distaste
I fold my towel with what grace I can,
Not young and not renewable, but man.

from
WORMWOOD
1966

*and a great star fell from heaven, burning
as it were a torch; and it fell on the
third part of the rivers and upon the fountains
of waters; and the name of the star is
called Wormwood; and the third part of
the waters became wormwood; and many men
died of the waters, because they were made
bitter.*

Apocalypse: Ch. 8, vv. 10 and 11

Beloved,

A little of what we have found . . .

It is certain that maturity and peace are to be sought through ordeal after ordeal, and it seems that the search continues until we fail. We reach out after each new beginning, penetrating our context to know ourselves, and our knowledge increases until we recognise again (more profoundly each time) our pain, indignity and triviality. This bitter cup is offered, heaped with curses, and we must drink or die. And even though we drink we may also die, if every drop of bitterness — that rots the flesh — is not transmuted. (Certainly the individual plight is hideous, each torturing each, but we are guilty, seeing this, to believe that our common plight is only hideous. Believing so, we make it so: pigs in a slaughter-yard that turn and savage each other in a common desperation and disorder.) Death, either way, is guilt and failure. But if we drink the bitterness and can transmute it and continue, we resume in candour and doubt the only individual joy — the restored necessity to learn. Sensing a wider scope, a more penetrating harmony, we begin again in a higher innocence to grow toward the next ordeal.

Love also, it seems, will continue until we fail: in the sensing of the wider scope, in the growth toward it, in the swallowing and absorption of bitterness, in the resumed innocence . . .

Open this and you will see
A waste, a nearly naked tree
That will not rest till it is bare,
But shivers, shivers in the air
Scraping at its yellow leaves.
Winter, when the tempest heaves,
It riots in the heaven-sent
Convulsions of self-punishment.

What cannot rest till it is bare,
Though branches crack and fibres tear?

WORMWOOD

I have dreamt it again: standing suddenly still
In a thicket, among wet trees, stunned, minutely
Shuddering, hearing a wooden echo escape.

A mossy floor, almost colourless, disappears
In depths of rain among the tree shapes.
I am straining, tasting that echo a second longer.

If I can hold it . . . familiar if I can hold it . . .
A black tree with a double trunk — two trees
Grown into one — throws up its blurred branches.

The two trunks in their infinitesimal dance of growth
Have turned completely about one another, their join
A slowly twisted scar, that I recognise . . .

A quick arc flashes sidewise in the air,
A heavy blade in flight. A wooden stroke:
Iron sinks in the gasping core.

                              I will dream it again.

MASK OF LOVE

Mask of Love,
Do you turn to us for peace?
Me, flinching from your stare?
Her, whose face you bear?

Remember how we have climbed
The peaks of stress and stood
Wearily, again
And again, face to face
Across the narrow abyss.

Remember
That our very bodies lack peace:
In tiny darknesses
The skin angrily flames,
Nerve gropes for muscle
Across the silent abyss.

You have seen our nocturnal
Suicidal dance:
She, bent on some tiny mote;
I, doubled in laughter,
Clasping my paunch in grief
For the world in a speck of dust;
Between us, the fuming abyss.

Dumb vapours pour
Where the mask of Love appears,
Reddening, and disappears.

THE SECRET GARDEN

The place is growing difficult. Flails of bramble
Crawl into the lawn; on every hand
Glittering, toughened branches drink their dew.
Tiny worlds, drop by drop, tremble
On thorns and leaves; they will melt away.
The silence whispers around us:
Wither, wither, visible, invisible!

A child stands an instant at my knee.
His mouth smells of energy, light as light.
I touch my hand to his pearl flesh, taking strength.
He stands still, absorbing in return
The first taint. Immaculate, the waiting
Kernel of his brain.
How set him free, a son, toward the sour encounter?

Children's voices somewhere call his name.
He runs glittering into the sun, and is gone
. . . I cultivate my garden for the dew:
A rasping boredom funnels into death!
The sun climbs, a creature of one day,
And the dew dries to dust.
My hand strays out and picks off one sick leaf.

FIRST LIGHT

A prone couple still sleeps.
Light ascends like a pale gas
Out of the sea: dawn-
Light, reaching across the hill
To the dark garden. The grass
Emerges, soaking with grey dew.

Inside, in silence, an empty
Kitchen takes form, tidied and swept,
Blank with marriage — where shrill
Lover and beloved have kept
Another vigil far
Into the night, and raved and wept.

Upstairs a whimper or sigh
Comes from an open bedroom door
And lengthens to an ugly wail
— A child enduring a dream
That grows, at the first touch of day,
Unendurable.

REMEMBERING OLD WARS

What clamped us together? When each night fell we lay down
In the smell of decay and slept, our bodies leaking,
Limp as the dead, breathing that smell all night.

Then light prodded us awake, and adversity
Flooded up from inside us as we laboured upright
Once more to face the hells of circumstance.

And so on, without hope of change or peace.
Each dawn, like lovers recollecting their purpose,
We would renew each other with a savage smile.

Je t'adore

The other props are gone.
Sighing in one another's
Iron arms, propped above nothing,
We praise Love the limiter.

from
NIGHTWALKER AND OTHER POEMS
1968

OUR MOTHER

Tall windows full of sea light,
Two women and a child in tears
Silent among screens and flowers,
The ward a quiet zone of air.

The girl whimpers in bed, remote
Under the anaesthetic still.
She sleeps on her new knowledge, a bride
With bowels burning and disarrayed.

She dreams a red Gorgon-mask
Warped in the steel kidney dish,
The tender offals of her core
Worming around the raw stare.

Her mother watches, struck dumb.
Tears of recognition run
For the stranger, daughter, self, on whom
In fascination her eyes feed,

As mine on her — a revenant,
A rain-worn, delicate
Stone shape that has looked long
Into that other face direct.

In the next bed, dying of age,
The carrier of all our harm
Turns on us an emptiness
Of open mouth and damp eyes.

All three women, two in my care,
The third beyond all care, in tears.
Living, dying, I meet their stare
Everywhere, and cannot move.

OFFICE FOR THE DEAD

The grief-chewers enter, their shoes hard on the marble,
In white lace and black skirts, books held to their loins.
A silver pot tosses in its chains as they assemble
About the coffin, heavy under its cloth, and begin.

Back and forth, each side in nasal unison
Against the other, their voices grind across her body.
We watch, kneeling like children, and shrink as their Church
Latin chews our different losses into one

— All but certain images of her pain that will not,
In the coarse process, pass through the cloth and hidden boards
To their peace in the shroud; that delay, still real —

High thin shoulders — eyes boring out of the dusk —
Wistful misshapenness — a stripped, dazzling mouth —
Her frown as she takes the candle pushed into her hands
In the last crisis, propped up, dying with worry.

Sanctus. We listen with bowed heads to the thrash of chains
Measuring the silence. The pot gasps in its smoke.
An animal of metal, dragging itself and breathing . . .

BALLYDAVID PIER

Noon. The luminous tide
Climbs through the heat, covering
Grey shingle. A film of scum
Searches first among litter,
Cloudy with (I remember)
Life; then crystal-clear shallows
Cool on the stones, silent
With shells and claws, white fish bones;
Farther out a bag of flesh,
Foetus of goat or sheep,
Wavers below the surface.

Allegory forms of itself:
The line of life creeps upward
Replacing one world with another,
The welter of its advance
Sinks down into clarity,
Slowly the more foul
Monsters of loss digest . . .

Small monster of true flesh
Brought forth somewhere
In bloody confusion and error
And flung into bitterness,
Blood washed white:
Does that structure satisfy?

The ghost tissue hangs unresisting
In allegorical waters,
Lost in self-search
— A swollen blind brow

Humbly crumpled over
Budding limbs, unshaken
By the spasms of birth or death.

The Angelus. Faint bell-notes
From some church in the distance
Tremble over the water.
It is nothing. The vacant harbour
Is filling; it will empty.
The misbirth touches the surface
And glistens like quicksilver.

LANDSCAPE AND FIGURE

A man stoops low on the overcast plain. He is earthing
Or uprooting among heavy leaves. In the whole field
One dull poppy burns, on the drill by his boots.

The furrows yield themselves to his care. He does not
Lift his head; and would not, though the blight
Breathed on his fields out of the low clouds.

The blight breathes, or does not, invisibly,
As it will. Stalks still break into scattered flower.
Tissue forms about purpose as about seed.

He works toward the fruit of Adam. It darkens the plain,
Its seed a huge brain. The protecting flesh
When it falls will melt away in a kind of mud.

MUSEUM

Out of doors the season dies, a fountain
Ruffles in the wind. The great Museum
Squats closer on its hoard and will not move.
Its blocks of granite, speechless with fatigue,
Imply the slithering pit, the shapelessly-
Adjusting matter of the rubbish heap.

Webs of corridors and numbered rooms
Catch the onward turbulence of forms
Against museum technique; flux disperses
In order everywhere, in glass cases
Or draped or towering in enormous gloom.
Human voice and footstep die.

A dozen tiny coarse clay animals
Picked from a midden — hook-winged geese or hawks,
A bull with pitted head free to move —
Squat blindly. The remote curator speaks:
'In the beginning there were toys, implying love . . .'
Voice and footstep die away.

TRAVELLER

Behind me my children vanish, left asleep
In their strange bed, in apple-tasted night.
I drive from worry to worry, to where my wife
Struggles for her breath in a private room.

An hour to midnight, and the traps of self
Are open for eighty solitary miles ahead,
In the swerving ditch, in the flash of tree-trunks and hedges.

The brain, woken to itself and restless,
Senses their black mouths muttering in the darkness:
Phrases, echoes of feeling, from other journeys
To bait and confuse the predatory will
And draw it aside, muttering in absent response,
Down stale paths in the dark to a stale lair,
In brainless trance, where it can treadle and chew
Old pangs blunter and smoother, old self-mutilations.

Far ahead on the road the lamps caught something.
A cat. A bird. Mesmerised. It moved,
Eating. It rose slowly, white furred, and flew
Up into the dark. An owl! My heart
Stood still. I had forgotten the very existence . . .

WESTLAND ROW

We came to the outer light down a ramp in the dark
Through eddying cold gusts and grit, our ears
Stopped with noise. The hands of the station clock
Stopped, or another day vanished exactly.
The engine departing hammered slowly overhead.
Dust blowing under the bridge, we stooped slightly
With briefcases and books and entered the wind.

The savour of our days restored, dead
On nostril and tongue. Drowned in air,
We stepped on our own traces, not on stone,
Nodded and smiled distantly and followed
Our scattering paths, not stumbling, not touching.

Until, in a breath of benzine from a garage-mouth,
By the Academy of Music coming against us,
She stopped an instant in her wrinkled coat
And ducked her childish cheek in the coat-collar
To light a cigarette: seeing nothing,
Thick-lipped, in her grim composure.

Daughterwife, look upon me.

FOLK WISDOM

Each year for a short season
The toads stare and wait
And clutch in their being
A shrieking without breath.
There is nothing but the harrow —
Everything speaks its approach;
Even blades of grass,
Flower stems, are harrows' teeth,
Hideous, because they are
Parallel and in earth.

The men are shackling their horses
In the yard. They talk softly
About earth and seed.

Soon the toads will shriek —
Each, as he hears his neighbour,
Gathers all his strength.

And so the curse was lifted,
According to the tale;
One kiss, and a prince stood there
Where a toad had been.
It is possible . . . such a strain,
Under the kiss of the harrow,
Could suffice. As when a man
Clutches his ears, deafened
By his world, to find a jewel
Made of pain in his hands.

TARA

The mist hung on the slope, growing whiter
On the thin grass and dung by the mounds;
It hesitated at the dyke, among briars.

Our children picked up the wrapped flasks, capes and baskets
And we trailed downward among whins and thrones
In a muffled dream, guided by slender axe-shapes.

Our steps scattered on the soft turf, leaving
No trace, the childrens' voices like light.
Low in the sky behind us, a vast silver shield

Seethed and consumed itself in the thick ether.
A horse appeared at the rampart like a ghost,
And tossed his neck at ease, with a hint of harness.

THE SHOALS RETURNING
In memory of Gerry Flaherty, drowned 1959

I dip the oar and lean
Supported and opposed
On the green flesh of a wave.
The ocean depth swallows
My strength like a stone.

A corpse balanced among
Striped fathoms turns
Over face upward.

He comes from the sea
Down at the gorge-mouth
Slow as a floating stick
A light boat is borne
Into the hall of rock.
It edges to a slope of stone
And washes back and forth,
Treading the watery floor.
Faint strokes of the oars
Echo in the chasm.
A man in cap and boots
Throws his coat onto the slip:
He stoops and flings out
The body of a cod,
A sheaf of slithering mackerel,
A handfull of crabs' claws.

*

He passes on the cliff road
Against depths of marine light:
Narrow-necked, erect,
Averse, in coarse grey jacket
And trousers, wrists loose, his eyes
Black points of spray. A slow
Harsh thunder from below —
The Wave of Tóim snarls
With distance, shudders in its caves;
It writhes milkily,
A ragged foam-web joining
And unlinking among the rocks,
Seizes the cliff in white
Turmoil, sighs and crumbles
— Breakers against breakers —
Chewing the solid earth.

He sings
A voice rises flickering
From palatal darkness, a thin yell
Straining erect, checked
In glottal silence. The song
Articulates and pierces.

A boot scrapes the floor. Live eyes
Shine, each open on its rock,
In horn-darkness of paraffin,
Rope and gas cylinders.
Wet glasses of stout
Cling to boxes and casks;
Men, sunk in shade, listen
On their benches, bodies tainted
With cold sea wind.

Their eyes respond; squat
Entities turn in cranial darkness
In the ravenous element
At the innermost turn of the shell.

He sings at the back of the shop:
Slit eyes above high cheeks, jaws
Drawn back, teeth bared to the voice.
In the exercise of his gift
His throat constricts; speech,
Human proportion, distort
Slightly to permit the cry
That can prepare the spirit
To turn softly and be eaten
In the smell of brine and blood.

Dark shell breath, tatters of mist
And sea-foam blown from the waves
Fly inland. Soiled feathers scatter
On the shingle. Sea birds' fleeting
Bodies pierce the wind.

He returns

In that Autumn, after fifteen
Years, a new direction
Loosened the seed in the depths;
The mackerel shoals reappeared
And the water in the Sound shivered.

The boats waited at Smerwyck,
Black-skinned, crook-backed,
On the grass by the drying boat-slip;
The rocky knife-sharp shore
Drained bare: crayfish stared:

Brutal torso of conger
Slid through a choked slit —
Naked savagery
On which, when the eyes lift,
An infinite sheen alights,
A sheet of blinding water
Pierced by black points of rock.
By nightfall the bay ran cold
With the distant returning tide
Under the wall of Mount Brandon.
The clefts brimmed in darkness.

*

Booted spirits are at work;
A heavy step scrapes
On the slip; a boat tosses
With a feathery splash. They vanish
Over covered razors of rock
And move out with crisp
Tangles of net, vague
Oar-voices, a fading
Taint of canvas and rope,
Past cliff wall and washed rocks
Over meshes of hissing foam.
They cross into the Sound
And climb the swell blindly,
Dropping in dark valleys.

Nets are shaken out
And swallowed into the sea.
The lines reach far down
And open everywhere
Among the haunted levels.

A million shadows here
Pursue their staring will
Along echoing cold paths.
The delicate veil of garottes
Drags, scarcely breathing,
Then touches a living shoal.
Fierce bodies leap into being
Strangling all over the net,
An anguish of shivering lives.
They gather weight, shudder
By shudder, and — gazing about them —
Turn to unbearable stone.

He disappears
Dawn opened on a jewel
Twisting in the sea
Under the empty boat
— A net of suffocated fish
Tied fast to the seat board
Pulling the head down in the waves:
Two thousand mackerel
Torn from the intense shoal,
Stopped dead and gathered up
With mourning devils' mouths
And scales and rigid eyes
In a clustre shaped by its own
Weight against the diamond-
Meshes of its bonds.
The drowned men have fallen away
Through the water and separated
With slow hair in the calm.
Now their jewel drifts
— Until it rots to pieces —
For anyone to find.

*

A withered man, a coat
Across his shoulders, watches
From the cliff over the gorge
— A black outcrop thrust
Partly out of the soil
Into the salt wind.
The shale-grass shivers around him.
He turns a shrunken mask
Of cheekbone and jawbone
And pursed ancient mouth
On the sea surface.
A windswept glitter of light
Murmurs toward the land.
His eyes, out of tortoise lids,
Assess the crystalline plasm,
Formations of water
Under falls of air.

BEFORE SLEEP

It is time for bed. The cups and saucers are gathered
And stacked in the kitchen, the tray settled
With your tablets, a glass, a small jug of orange.
Are the windows shut, and all the doors locked?

I pass near the desk in my room and stand a minute
Looking down the notes I made this morning.
Yes: tomorrow it might do to begin . . .
Thunder whispers far-off among my papers.

The wall opposite is blank but alive
— Standing water over sunken currents.
The currents pursue their slow eddies through the house
Scarcely loosening as yet the objects of our love.

Soon the Falls will thunder, our love's detritus
Slide across the brim seriatim, glittering,
And vanish, swallowed into that insane
White roar. Chaos. All battered, scattered.

Yes: in the morning I will put on the cataract,
Give it veins, clutching hands, the short shriek of thought.

MAGNANIMITY
(for Austin Clarke's seventieth birthday)

        'So I forgot
His enmity.'
                             Green abundance
Last summer in Coole Park. A stone hearth
Surviving; a grassy path by the orchard wall.

You stared through chicken-wire at the initials
Cut in Lady Gregory's tree, scars grown thick.
Overhead a breath passed magniloquently through the leaves,

Branches swayed and sank. You turned away and said
Coole might be built again as a place for poets.
Through the forbidden tree magnanimity passed.

I am sure that there are no places for poets,
Only changing habitations for verse to outlast.
Your own house, isolated by a stream, exists

For your use while you live — like your body and your world.
Helpless commonness encroaches, chews the soil,
Squats ignobly. Within, consciousness intensifies:

Sharp small evils magnify into Evil,
Pity and mockery suggest some idea of Good,
Fright stands up stiffly under pain of death.

Houses shall pass away, and all give place
To signposts and chicken-wire.
                         A tree stands.
Pale cress persists on a shaded stream.

THE POET EGAN O'RAHILLY, HOMESICK IN OLD AGE

He climbed to his feet in the cold light, and began
The decrepit progress again, blown along the cliff road,
Bent with curses above the shrew his stomach.

The salt abyss poured through him, more raw
With every laboured, stony crash of the waves:
His teeth bared at their voices, that incessant dying.

Iris leaves bent on the ditch, unbent,
Shivering in the wind: leaf-like spirits
Chattered at his death-mark as he passed.

He pressed red eyelids; aliens crawled
Breaking princely houses in their jaws;
Their metal faces reared up, chewing at light.

'Princes overseas, who slipped away
In your extremity, no matter where I travel
I find your great houses like stopped hearts.

Likewise your starving children — though I nourish
Their spirit, and my own, on the lists of praises
I make for you still in the cooling den of my craft.

Our enemies multiply. They have recruited the sea:
Last night, the West's rhythmless waves destroyed my sleep;
This morning, winkle and dogfish persisting in the stomach . . .'

'TO AUTUMN'

Insect beads crawl on the warm soil,
Black carapaces; brittle harvest spiders
Clamber weightlessly among dry roots
In soundless bedlam. He sits still writing
At the edge of the wheatfield, a phantasm of flesh
                              while thy hook
       Spares . . .
Ripened leagues, a plain of odorous seed,
Quiet scope, season of mastery,
The last of peace. Along ethereal summits,
A gleam of disintegrating materials
Held a frail instant at unearthly heights.

DEATH IN ILIUM
(In Yeats's centenary year)

Attention and power relax,
Truth deserts the body:
Hector among his books
Drops dead in the dust.

The tireless shadow-eaters
Close in with tough nose
And pale fang to expose
Fibre, weak flesh, speech organs.

They eat, but cannot eat.
Dog-faces in his bowels,
Bitches at his face,
He grows whole and remote.

SOFT TOY

I am soiled with the repetition of your loves and hatreds
    And other experiments. You do not hate me,
Crumpled in my corner. You do not love me,
    A small heaped corpse. My face of beaten fur
Responds as you please: if you do not smile
    It does not smile; to impatience or distaste
It answers blankness, beyond your goodwill
    — Blank conviction, beyond your understanding or mine.

I lie limp with use and re-use, listening.
    Loose ends of conversations, hesitations,
Half-beginnings that peter out in my presence,
    Are enough. I understand, with a flame of shame
Or a click of ease or joy, inert. Knowledge
    Into resignation: the process drives deeper,
Grows clearer, eradicating chance growths of desire
    — And colder: all possibilities of desire.

My button-brown hard eyes fix on your need
    To grow, as you crush me with tears and throw me aside.
Most they reflect, but something absorb — brightening
    In response, with energy, to the energy of your changes.
Clutched tightly through the night, held before you,
    Ragged and quietly crumpled, as you thrust, are thrust,
In dull terror into your opening brain,
    I face the dark with eyes that cannot close
    — The cold, outermost points of your will, as you sleep.
    Between your tyrannous pressure and the black
Resistance of the void my blankness hardens
    To a blunt probe, a cold pitted grey face.

LEAF-EATER

On a shrub in the heart of the garden,
On an outer leaf, a grub twists
Half its body, a tendril,
This way and that in blind
Space: no leaf or twig
Anywhere in reach; then gropes
Back on itself and begins
To eat its own leaf.

NIGHTWALKER

The greater part must be content to be
as though they had not been.

Mindful of the
    shambles of the day
But mindful, under the
    blood's drowsy humming,
Of will that gropes for
    structure — nonetheless
Not unmindful of
    the madness without,
The madness within (the
    book of reason slammed
Open, slammed shut)
    we presume to say:

I

I only know things seem and are not good.

A brain in the dark, and bones, out exercising
Shadowy flesh; fitness for the soft belly,
Fresh air for lungs that take no pleasure any longer.
The smell of gardens under suburban lamplight,
Clipped privet, a wall blotted with shadows
— Monsters of ivy squat in lunar glare.
                    There, above the roofs,
It hangs, like a fat skull, or the pearl knob
Of a pendulum at the outermost reach of its swing,
Motionless. It is about to detach
Its hold on the upper night, for the return.
                   Aye, I remember talk of it,
Though only a child. Not far from here it passed through
                      — remorseless cratered face
Swift as the wind: a bludgeon tears free
From the world's bones, spikes breaking off
— Millions of little sharp limbs, jets of blood
Petrified in terror, jetted screams —
Then plunges upward far into the darkness —
                It meant little to me then,
Though I remember playing in the silence
When the rain of fragments dropped in the streets afterward
— Bone-splinters, silvery slivers of screams,
Blood-splinters rattling, like crimson flint.
               There it hangs,
A mask of grey dismay sagging open
In the depths of torture, moron voiceless moon.
That dark area, the mark of Cain.

*

My shadow twists about my feet in the light
Of every passing street-lamp. Will-o'-the-wisp
In a bay window; a shadow slumped in the corner
Of a living-room, in blue trance, buried
Alive, two blank eyes. On a tiny screen
Mouths open and close, and bodies move
Obliquely and stoop, flickering —
                                        embalmers
In eery light underground; their arms
Toil in silence.
                    A laboratory
Near Necropolis. It is midnight.
A shade enters,
                    patrolling the hive of his brain.
                              Window after window,
The same unearthly light consumes pitilessly.
Surely we can never die, sick spirits . . .
                              The minions stretch at rest,
Pale entities wound in a drowsy humming
At the brink of sleep. They snuggle in their cells
Faintly luminous, like grubs — abdominal
Body-juices and paper-thin shells, in their thousands,
In the smashable wax, o moon!
                              Musing thus,
I stroll upon my way, a vagabond
Tethered. My shadow twists at their feet.

                              *

I must lie down with them all soon and sleep,
And rise with them again when the new dawn
Has touched our pillows and our wet pallor
And roused us. We'll come scratching in our waistcoats
Down to the kitchen for a cup of tea;

103

Then with our briefcases, through wind or rain,
Past our neighbours' gardens — Melrose, Bloomfield —
To wait at the station, fluttering our papers,
Palping the cool wind, discussing and murmuring.
                              Is it not right to serve
Our banks and businesses and government
As together we develop our community
On clear principles, with no fixed ideas?
And (twitching our thin umbrellas) acceptable
That during a transitional period
Development should express itself in forms
Without principle, based on fixed ideas —
                              Robed in spattered iron
At the harbour mouth she stands, Productive Investment,
And beckons the nations through our gold half-door:
Lend me your wealth, your cunning and your drive,
Your arrogant refuse;
                              let my people serve them
Bottled fury in our new hotels,
While native businessmen and managers
Drift with them, chatting, over to the window
To show them our growing city, give them a feeling
Of what is possible; our labour pool,
The tax concessions to foreign capital,
How to get a nice estate though German,
Even collect some of our better young artists.
                              Morose condemnation . . .
It is a weakness, and turns on itself.
                              Clean bricks
Are made of mud; we need them for our tower.

*

Spirit-skeletons are straggling into view
From the day's depths. You can pick them out
In the night sky, with a little patience:
                        Pale influences . . .
The wakeful Twins,
                        Bruder und Schwester
— Two young Germans I had in this morning
Wanting to transfer investment income;
The sister a business figurehead, her brother
Otterfaced, with exasperated smiles
Assuming — pressing until he achieved — response.
Handclasp; I do not exist; I cannot take
My eyes from their pallor. A red glare
Plays on their faces, livid with little splashes
Of blazing fat. The oven door closes.
                        All about and above me
The officials on the corridors or in their rooms
Work, or overwork, with mixed motives
Or none. We dwell together in urgency;
Dominate, entering middle age; subserve,
Aborting vague tendencies with buttery smiles.
Among us, behind locked doors, the ministers
Are working, with a sureness of touch found early
In the nation's birth — the blood of enemies
And brothers dried on their hide long ago.
Dragon old men, upright and stately and blind,
Or shuffling in the corridor finding a key,
Their youth cannot die in them; it will be found
Beating with violence when their bodies rot.
                        What occupies them
As they sit in their rooms? What they already are?
Shadow-flesh . . . claimed by pattern still living,
Linked into constellations with their dead . . .

Look! The Wedding Group:
The Groom, the Best Man, the Fox, and their three ladies
— A tragic tale: soon, the story tells,
Enmity sprang up between them, and the Fox
Took to the wilds. Then, to the Groom's sorrow,
His dear friend left him also, vowing hatred.
So they began destroying the Groom's substance
And he sent out to hunt the Fox, but trapped
His friend instead; mourning, he slaughtered him.
Shortly, in his turn, the Groom was savaged
On a Sunday morning, no one knows by whom.
And look, over here, in the same quarter,
The Two Executioners — Groom and Weasel —
'77' burning into each brow;
And look, the vivid Weasel there again,
Dancing crookbacked under the Player King
— A tragicomical tale:
                        how the Fox, long after,
Found a golden instrument one day,
A great complex gold horn, left at his door;
He examined it with little curiosity,
Wanting no gold or music, observed the mouthpiece,
Impossible to play with fox's lips,
And gave it with dull humour to his old enemy
The Weasel — who recognised the horn
Of the Player King, and bared his needle teeth.
He took it, hammered on it with a stick
And pranced about in blithe pantomime,
His head cocked to enjoy the golden clouts,
While the Fox from time to time nodded his mask.

II

The human taste grows faint.
                              It is gone,
Leaving a taste of self and laurel leaves
                              And rotted salt:
The gardens begin to smell of soaked sand
And half-stripped rocks in the dark. My bones obey
The sighing of the tide.
                              Another turning:
A cast-iron lamp-standard sheds yellow light
On the sea-wall; other lamps are lighting
Along a terrace of Victorian red brick.
Big snails glisten among roots of iris.
Not a breath of wind. Joyce's Martello tower
Rises into the dark near the Forty Foot
On a prow frozen to stone.
                              Crossing the road
I hear my footsteps echo back from the terrace.
                              A sheet of newspaper
Gleams yellowish in the gutter. The morning *Times*:
Our new young minister glares from a photograph
— On horseback, in hunting pinks, from a low angle,
Haunch on haunch. Snigger, and by God . . .
                              The tide is drawing back
From the promenade, far as the lamplight can reach,
Trickling under the weed, into night's cave.
                              Note the silence.
Light never strays there. Nothing has a shadow there.
When a wind blows there . . .
                              A rustle in the gutter:
The hair stirs! Stealing over the waters,
Through the smell of seaweed, a spectral stink of horse
And rider's sweat . . .

What's that, outside the light?

*

Watcher in the tower, be with me now
At your parapet, above the glare of the lamps.
Turn your milky spectacles on the sea
Unblinking; cock your ear.
                              A rich darkness
Alive with signals: lights flash and wink;
Little bells clonk in the channel near the rocks;
Howth twinkles across the bay; ship-lights move
By invisible sea-lanes; the Baily light
Flickers, as it sweeps the middle darkness,
On some commotion . . .
                              A dripping cylinder
Big as a ship's funnel, pokes into sight,
Picked out by the moon. Two blazing eyes.
Then a whole head. Shoulders of shadowy muscle
Lit from within by joints and bones of light.
Another head . . . animal, with nostrils straining
Open, red as embers; goggle-eyes;
A spectral whinny! Forehoofs scrape at the night,
A rider grunts and urges.
                              Father of Authors!
It is himself! In silk hat and jowls,
Accoutred in stern jodhpurs! The sonhusband
Coming in his power: mounting to glory
On his big white harse!
                              He climbs the dark
To his mansion in the sky, to take his place
In the influential circle — a new sign:
                              Foxhunter.

                              Subjects will find
The going hard but rewarding. You may give offence
But this should pass. Marry the Boss's daughter.

The newspaper settles down in the gutter again:
                    THE ARCHBISHOP ON MARRIAGE
NEW MOVES TO RESTORE THE LANGUAGE
                              THE NEW IRELAND . . .
                    still awkward in the saddle
But able and willing for the foul ditch.
You'll sit as well as any at the kill,
Dark brother. What matter what iron Fausts
Open the gates?
                    It is begun: the curs
Mill and yelp at your heel, backsnapping and grinning.
They eye your back. Watch the smile of the dog.
They wait your signal, the kick of dirt in the teeth,
To turn them, in the old miracle,
To a pack of lickspittles running as one.

                              *

The foot of the tower. An angle where the darkness
Is complete. The parapet is empty.
A backdrop of constellations, crudely done
And mainly unfamiliar; they are arranged
To suggest a chart of the brain. Music far off.
In the part of the little harbour that can be seen
The moon is reflected in low water.
Beyond, the lamps on the terrace.
                              The music fades.
                    Snuggle into the skull.
Total darkness wanders among my bones.
Lung-tips flutter. Wavelets lap the shingle.

From the vest's darkness, smell of my body:
Chalk dust and flowers . . .
Faint brutality. Shoes creak in peace.
Brother Burke flattens his soutane
Against the desk.
And the authorities
Used the National Schools to try to conquer
The Irish national spirit, at the same time
Exterminating what they called our 'jargon'
— The Irish language; in which Saint Patrick, Saint Bridget
And Saint Columcille taught and prayed!
Edmund Ignatius Rice founded our Order
To provide schools that were national in more than name.
Pupils from our schools played their part,
As you know, in the fight for freedom. And you will be called
In your different ways — to work for the native language,
To show your love by working for your country.
Today there are Christian Brothers' boys
Everywhere in the Government — the present Taoiseach
Sat where one of you is sitting now.
It wasn't long before Her Majesty
Gave us the famine — the starvation, as Bernard Shaw,
A godless writer, called it more accurately.
A hand is laid on my brow.
A voice breathes: You will ask are we struck dumb
By the unsimplifiable. Take these . . .
Bread of certainty; scalding soup of memories,
For my drowsy famine — martyrs in a dish
Of scalding tears: food of dragon men
And my own dragon half. Fierce pity!
The Blessed Virgin smiles
From her waxed pedestal, like young Victoria;
A green snake wriggles under her heel
Beside a vase of tulips.

                    Adolescents,
Celibates, we offer up our vows
To God and Ireland in Her name, grateful
That by our studies here they may not lack
Civil servants in a state of grace.
                              A glass partition rattles
In the draught. Rain against the windows.
A shiver clothes the flesh
                              bittersweet.
                    A seamew passes over,
Whingeing:
          Eire, Eire . . . is there none
To hear? Is all lost?
                    Not yet all; a while still
Your voice . . .
          Alas, I think I will dash myself
At the stones. I will became a wind on the sea
Or a wave of the sea again, or a sea sound.
At the first light of the sun I stirred on my rock;
I have seen the sun go down at the end of the world;
Now I fly across the face of the moon.
                    A dying language echoes
Across a century's silence.
                    It is time,
Lost soul, I turned for home.
                    Sad music steals
Over the scene.
          Hesitant, cogitating, exit.

III

Home and beauty.
                  Her dear shadow on the blind,
The breadknife . . . She was slicing and buttering
A loaf of bread. My heart stopped. I starved for speech.
I believe now that love is half persistence,
A medium in which, from change to change,
Understanding may be gathered.
                    The return:
                  Virgin most pure, bright
In the dregs of the harbour: moon of my dismay,
Quiet as oil, enormous in her shaggy pool.
Her brightness, reflected on earth, in heaven,
Consumes my sight. Gradually, as my brain
At a great distance swims in the steady light,
Scattered notes, scraps of newspaper, photographs,
Begin to flow unevenly toward the pool
And gather into a book before her stare.
Her mask darkens as she reads, to my faint terror,
But she soon brightens a little, and smiles wanly:
                  It was a terrible time,
Nothing but sadness and horrors of one kind and another.
We came to take the waters. The sun shone brightly,
Which was very pleasant, and made it less gloomy,
Though my tears flowed again and again. When I drank
I felt my patience and trust coming back.
From time to time it seems that everything
Is breaking down; but we must never despair.
There are times it is all part of a meaningful drama
That begins in the grey mists of antiquity
And reaches through the years to unknown goals
In the consciousness of man, which is very soothing.

A wind sighs. The pool
Shivers: the tide at the turn. Odour of lamplight,
Sour soil, the sea bed, passes like a ghost
— The hem of her invisible garment.

                                        Our mother
Rules on high, queenlike, pale with control.
                        Hatcher of peoples!
Incline from your darkness into mine!
I stand at the ocean's edge, my head fallen back
Heavy with your control, and oppressed!

                          *

That mad stare — the pulse hisses in my ear —
I am an arrow piercing the void, unevenly
As I correct and correct, but swift as thought.
I arrive, enveloped in blinding silence.

                                  No wind   stirs
On the dust floor. Far as the eye can see
Rock needles stand up from the plain; the horizon
A ring of sharp mountains like broken spikes.
Hard bluish light beats down, to kill
Any bodily thing — but a million dead voices hide
From it in the dust, without hope of peace.
(A cloud bursts from the ground, rock fragments scatter
In total silence.) A true desert, naked
To every peril. The shadows are alive:
They scuttle and flicker among the rock needles,
Squat and suck the dry juice, inspect
The eggs of shadow beneath the surface, twitching
Madly in their cells.

                    The earth, at the full,
Hangs in blue splendour in the sky.

                              I believe I have heard
Of this place.
              In the mind darkness tosses:
The light deceives. A vivid ghost sea
Quivers and dazzles for miles.
                              Let us take the waters.
Stoop down, run the fingers along the brink.
It has a human taste, but sterile; odourless.
Massed human wills . . .
                    A dust plain flickering . . .
I think this is the Sea of Disappointment.

RITUAL OF DEPARTURE

A man at the moment of departure, turning
To leave, treasures some stick of furniture
With slowly blazing eyes, or the very door
Broodingly with his hand as it falls shut.

*

Open the soft string that clasps in series
A dozen silver spoons, and spread them out,
Matched perfectly, one maker and to the year:
                              brilliance in use that fell
Open before the first inheritor.

A stag crest stares from the soft solid silver
And grimaces, with fat cud-lips but jaws
That could crack bones.
                              The stag heart stumbles.
He rears at bay, slavering silver; rattles
A trophied head among my gothic rocks.

*

Stones of a century and a half ago.
The same city distinct in the same air,
More open in an earlier evening light.
Dublin under the Georges . . .
                              stripped of Parliament,
Lying powerless in sweet-breathing death-ease
                              after forced Union.
Under a theatre of swift-moving cloud
Domes, pillared, in the afterglow —
A portico, beggars moving on the steps —

A horserider locked in soundless greeting,
Bowed among dogs and dung; the panelled vista
Closing on pleasant smoke-blue far-off hills.

*

The ground opens. Pale wet potatoes
Break into light. The black soil falls from their flesh,
From the hands that tear them up and spread them out
In fresh disorder, perishable roots to eat.
     The fields vanish in rain
Among white rock and red bog — saturated
High places traversed by spring sleet
Or thrust up in summer through the thin wind
Into pounding silence. Farther south: cattle,
Wheat, salmon glistening, the sea.
Landscape with ancestral figures . . . names
Settling and intermixing on the earth,
The seed in slow retreat, through time and blood,
Into bestial silence.
     Faces sharpen and grow blank,
With eyes for nothing.
     And their children's children
Venturing to disperse, some came to Dublin
To vanish in the city lanes.
     I saw the light
Enter from the laneway, through the scullery
To the foot of the stairs, creep across grey floorboards,
Sink in plush in the staleness of an inner room.

I scoop at the earth, and sense famine, a first
Sourness in the clay. The roots tear softly.

PHOENIX PARK

The Phœnix builds the Phœnix' nest.
Love's architecture is his own.

I

One stays or leaves. The one who returns is not
The one, etcetera. And we are leaving.
You are quiet and watchful, this last visit.
We pass the shapes of cattle blurred by moisture;
A few deer lift up their wet horns from the grass;

A smoke-soft odour of graves . . . our native damp.
A twig with two damp leaves drops on the bonnet
From the upper world, trembling; shows us its clean
Fracture and vanishes, snatched off by the wind:
Droplets of moisture shudder on the windscreen.

— You start at the suddenness, as though it were
Your own delicate distinct flesh that had snapped.
What was in your thoughts . . . saying, after a while,
I write you nothing, no love songs, any more?
Fragility echoing fragilities . . .

The Chapelizod Gate. Dense trees on our right,
Sycamores and chestnuts around the entrance
To St. Mary's Hospital. Under their shade
I entered long ago, took the twisting paths
To find you by the way of hesitation.

You lay still, brilliant with illness, behind glass;
I stooped and tasted your life until you woke,
And your body's fever leaped out at my mind.
There's a fever now that eats everything,
— Everything but the one positive dream.

That dream . . . it is something I might offer you,
Sorry it is not anything for singing;
Your body would know that it is positive
— Everything you know you know bodily.
And the preparation also . . . Take them both.

The preparation
Near a rounded wooded hillock, where a stream
Drains under the road, inside Islandbridge Gate,
A child stooped to the grass, picking and peeling
And devouring mushrooms straight out of the ground:
Death-pallor in their dry flesh, the taste of death.

Later, in freezing darkness, I came alone
To the railings round the Pond; whispered *Take me,
I am nothing.* But the words hovered, their sense
Revealing opposite within opposite.
Understanding moved, a silent bright discus.

As, when I walked this glimmering road, it did
Once, between night-trees. The stars seemed in my grasp,
Changing places among the naked branches
— Thoughts drawing into order under night's skull.
But something moved on the path: faint, sweet breathing —

A woman stood, thin and tired, in a light dress,
And interrupted kindly, in vague hunger.
Her hand rested for a moment on my sleeve.
I studied her and saw shame does not matter,
Nor kindness when there's no answering hunger

And passed by; her eyes burned . . . So equipped to learn
I found you, in feverish sleep, where you lay.
Midsummer, and I had tasted your knowledge,
My flesh blazing in yours; Autumn, I had learned
Giving without tearing is not possible.

*

The Furry Glen: grass sloping down to the lake,
Where she stooped in her Communion finery,
Our first-born, Sara in innocence, and plucked
Something out of the ground for us to admire.
The child smiled in her white veil, self-regarding.

II

We leave the Park through the Knockmaroon Gate and turn,
Remembering, downhill to the Liffey road
With the ache of dampness growing in our lungs.
Along river curves sunk under heavy scenes,
By the Strawberry Beds, under gravel slopes,

To sit drinking in a back bar in Lucan
At a glass table, under a staring light,
Talking of departure. You are uneasy;
I make signs on the surface with my wet glass
In human regret, but human certainty:

Whatever the ultimate grotesqueries
They'll have to root in more than this sour present.
The ordeal-cup, set at each turn, so far
We have welcomed, sour or sweet. What matter where
It waits for us next, if we will take and drink?

The dream
Look into the cup: the tissues of order
Form under your stare. The living surfaces
Mirror each other, gather everything
Into their crystalline world. Figure echoes
Figure faintly in the saturated depths;

Revealed by faint flashes of each other
They light the whole confines: a fitful garden . . .
A child plucks death and tastes it; a shade watches
Over him; the child fades and the shade, made flesh,
Stumbles on understanding, begins to fade,

Bequeathing a child in turn; women-shapes pass
Unseeing, full of knowledge, through each other
. . . All gathered. And the crystal so increases,
Eliciting in its substance from the dark
The slowly forming laws it increases by,

Laws of order I find I have discovered
Mainly at your hands . . . of failure and increase,
The stagger and recovery of spirit:
That life is hunger, hunger is for order,
And hunger satisfied brings on new hunger

Till there's nothing to come; — let the crystal crack
On some insoluble matter, then its heart
Shudders and accepts the flaw, adjusts on it
Taking new strength — given the positive dream;
Given, with your permission, undying love . . .

That, while the dream lasts, there's a total hunger
That gropes out disappearing just past touch,
A blind human face burrowing in the void,
Eating new tissue down into existence
Until every phantasm — all that can come —

Has roamed in flesh and vanished, or passed inward
Among the echoing figures to its place,
And this live world is emptied of its hunger
While the crystal world, undying, crowds with light,
Filling the cup . . . That there is one last phantasm

Who'll come painfully in old lewd nakedness
— Loose needles of bone coming out through his fat —
Groping with an opposite, equal hunger,
Thrusting a blind skull from its tatters of skin
As from a cowl, to smile in understanding

And total longing; aching to plant one kiss
In the live crystal as it aches with fullness,
And accommodate his body with that kiss;
But that forever he will pause, the final
Kiss ungiveable . . . Giving without tearing

Is not possible; to give totality
Is to be torn totally, a nothingness
Reaching out in stasis a pure nothingness.
— Therefore everlasting life, the unmoving
Stare of full desire. Given undying love . . .

*

I give them back not as your body knows them
— That flesh is finite, so in love we persist;
That love is to clasp simply, question fiercely;
That getting life we eat pain in each other —
But mental, in my fever — mere idea.

III

Our glasses drained, we finish and rise to go,
And stand again in the saturated air
Near the centre of the village, breathing in
Faint smells of chocolate and beer, fallen leaves
In the gutter, blank autumnal essences.

You wait a minute on the path, absently
— Against massed brown trees — tying a flimsy scarf
At your neck. Fair Ellinor. O Christ thee save.
And I taste a structure, ramshackle, ghostly,
Vanishing on my tongue, given and taken,

Distinct. A ghost of that ghost persists, structure
Without substance, all about us, in the air,
Among the trees, before us at the crossroads,
On the stone bridge, insinuating itself
Into being. Undying . . . And I shiver

Seeing your thoughtless delicate completeness.
Love, it is certain, continues till we fail,
Whenever (with your forgiveness) that may be
— At any time, now, totally, ordeal
Succeeding ordeal till we find some death,

Hoarding bitterness, or refusing the cup;
Then the vivifying eye clouds, and the thin
Mathematic tissues loosen, and the cup
Thickens, and order dulls and dies in love's death
And melts away in a hungerless no dream.

*

Fragility echoing fragilities
From whom I have had every distinctness
Accommodate me still, where — folded in peace
And undergoing with ghostly gaiety
Inner immolation, shallowly breathing —

You approach the centre by its own sweet light.
I consign my designing will stonily
To your flames. Wrapped in that rosy fleece, two lives
Burn down around one love, one flickering-eyed
Stone self becomes more patient than its own stone.

*

The road divides and we can take either way,
Etcetera. The Phoenix Park; Inchicore,
Passing Phoenix Street — the ways are one, sweet choise,
Our selves become our own best sacrifice.
Continue, so. We'll perish in each other.

IV

The tires are singing, cornering back and forth
In our green world again; into groves of trees,
By lake and open park, past the hospital.
The west ignites behind us; round one more turn
Pale light in the east hangs over the city:

An eighteenth century prospect to the sea —
River haze; gulls; spires glitter in the distance
Above faint multitudes. Barely audible
A murmur of soft, wicked laughter rises.
Dublin, the umpteenth city of confusion . . .

A theatre for the quick articulate,
The agonized genteel, their artful watchers . . .
Malice as entertainment. Asinine feast
Of sowthistles and brambles! And there dead men,
Half hindered by dead men, tear down dead beauty.

Return by the mental ways we have ourselves
Established, past visages of memory
Set at every turn: where we smiled and passed
Without a second thought, or stood in the rain
And whispered bitterly; where we roamed at night

Drunk in joyful love, looking for enemies
(They in our bodies — white handkerchief, white page,
Crimsoned with panic); where naked by firelight
We stood and rested from each other and took
Our burden from the future, eyes crystalline,

My past alive in you, a gift of tissue
Torn free from my life in an odour of books.
That room . . . The shapes of tiredness had assembled
Long ago in its four dark corners, before
You came, waiting, while you were everywhere.

One midnight at the starlit sill I let them
Draw near. Loneliness drew into order:
A thought of fires in the hearts of darknesses,
A darkness at the heart of every fire,
Darkness, fire, darkness, threaded on each other —

The orders of stars fixed in abstract darkness,
Darknesses of worlds sheltering in their light;
World darkness harbouring orders of cities,
Whose light at midnight harbours human darkness;
The human dark pierced by solitary fires . . .

Such fires as one I have seen gutter and fail
And, as it sank, reveal the fault in its heart
Opening on abstract darkness, where hunger
Came with gaping kiss over terrible wastes
–– Till the flames sprang up and blindness was restored.

Attracted from the night by my wakefulness
Certain half-dissolved — half-formed — beings loomed close:
A child with eaten features eating something —
Another, with unfinished features, in white —
They hold hands. A shadow bends to protect them.

The shadow tries to speak, but its tongue stumbles.
A snake out of the void moves in my mouth, sucks
At triple darkness. A few ancient faces
Detach and begin to circle. Deeper still,
Delicate distinct tissue begins to form,

NEW POEMS
1973

NOTES FROM THE LAND OF THE DEAD

hesitate, cease to exist, glitter again,
dither in and out of a mother liquid
on the turn, welling up from God knows what hole.

Dear God, if I had known how far and deep,
how long and cruel, I think my being
would have blanched: appalled.
                              How artless,
how loveless I was then! O dear, dear God,
the times I had in my disarray — cooped up
with the junk of centuries! The excitement,
underlining and underlining in that narrow room!
— dust (all that remained of something) settling
in the air over my pleasures.
                          Many a time
I have risen from my gnawed books
and prowled about, wrapped in a long grey robe,
and rubbed my forehead; reached for my instruments

— canister and kettle, the long-handled spoon,
metal vessels and delph; settled the flame,
blue and yellow; and, in abstracted hunger,
my book propped before me, eaten forkfulls
of scrambled egg and buttered fresh bread
and taken hot tea until the sweat stood out
at the roots of my hair!
                    Then, getting quietly ready
to go down quietly out of my mind,
I have lain down on the soiled divan
alert as though for a journey
and turned to things not right nor reasonable.
At such a time I wouldn't thank
the Devil himself to knock at my door.

                              *

The key, though I hardly knew it,
        already in my fist.
Falling. Mind darkening.
        Toward a ring of mouths.
Flushed.
            Time, distance,
        meaning nothing.
                    No matter.

                              *

I don't know how long I may have fallen
in terror of the uprushing floor
in my shell of solitude
when I became aware of certain rods of iron
laid down side by side, as if by giants,

in what had seemed the solid rock.
With what joy did I not hope, suddenly,
I might pass through unshattered
— to whatever Pit! But I fell foul at the last
and broke in a distress of gilt and silver,
scattered in a million droplets of
fright and loneliness . . .

                     So sunless.
That sour coolness . . . So far from the world and earth . . .
No bliss, no pain; dullness after pain.
A cistern-hiss . . . A thick tunnel stench
rose to meet me. Frightful. Dark nutrient waves.
And I knew no more.

                 When I came to,
the air I drifted in trembled around me
to a vast distance with sighs
— not from any great grief, but disturbed
by countless forms drifting as I did,
wavery albumen bodies
each burdened with an eye. Poor spirits!
How tentative and slack our search
along the dun shore whose perpetual hiss
breaks softly, and breaks again,
on endless broken shells! Stare as we will
with our red protein eyes, how few we discover
that are whole — a shell here and there
among so many — to slip into and grow blank!
Once more all faded.

                I was alone,
nearing the heart of the pit,
the light growing fitfully more bright.
A pale fume beat steadily through the gloom.
I saw, presently, it was a cauldron:

ceaselessly over its lip a vapour of forms
curdled, glittered and vanished. Soon I made out
a ring of mountainous beings, staring upward
with open mouths — naked ancient women.
Nothingness silted under their thighs
and over their limp talons. I confess
my heart, as I stole through to my enterprise,
hammered in fear.

       And then I raised my eyes
to that seemingly unattainable grill
through which I must return, carrying my prize.

*

How it was done — that that pot should now
be boiling before you . . .   I remember only snatches.
It must have been with utmost delicacy.
I was a mere plaything.

      But perhaps
you won't believe a word of this.
Yet by the five wounds of Christ
I struggled toward, by the five digits
of this raised hand, by this key
they hold now, glowing, and reach out with
to touch . . . you shall have . . .

 — what shall we not begin
    to have, on the
     count of

an egg of being

HEN WOMAN

The noon heat in the yard
smelled of stillness and coming thunder.
A hen scratched and picked at the shore.
It stopped, its body crouched and puffed out.
The brooding silence seemed to say 'Hush . . .'

The cottage door opened,
a black hole
in a whitewashed wall so bright
the eyes narrowed.
Inside, a clock murmured 'Gong . . .'

(I had felt all this before . . .)

She hurried out in her slippers
muttering, her face dark with anger,
and gathered the hen up jerking
languidly. Her hand fumbled.
Too late. Too late.

It fixed me with its pebble eyes
(seeing what mad blur?).
A white egg showed in the sphincter;
mouth and beak opened together;
and time stood still.

Nothing moved: bird or woman,
fumbled or fumbling — locked there
(as I must have been) gaping.

*

There was a tiny movement at my feet,
tiny and mechanical; I looked down.
A beetle like a bronze leaf
was inching across the cement,
clasping with small tarsi
a ball of dung bigger than its body.
The serrated brow pressed the ground humbly,
lifted in a short stare, bowed again;
the dung-ball advanced minutely,
losing a few fragments,
specks of staleness and freshness.

*

A mutter of thunder far off
— time not quite stopped.
I saw the egg had moved a fraction:
a tender blank brain
under torsion, a clean new world.

As I watched, the mystery completed.
The black zero of the orifice
closed to a point
and the white zero of the egg hung free,
flecked with greenish brown oils.

It slowly turned and fell.
Dreamlike, fussed by her splayed fingers,
it floated outward, moon-white,
leaving no trace in the air,
and began its drop to the shore.

*

I feed upon it still, as you see;
there is no end to that which,
not understood, may yet be noted
and hoarded in the imagination,
in the yolk of one's being, so to speak,
there to undergo its (quite animal) growth,
dividing blindly,
twitching, packed with will,
searching in its own tissue
for the structure
in which it may wake.
Something that had — clenched
in its cave — not been
now was: an egg of being.
Through what seemed a whole year it fell
— as it still falls, for me,
solid and light, the red gold beating
in its silvery womb,
alive as the yolk and white
of my eye; as it will continue
to fall, probably, until I die,
through the vast indifferent spaces
with which I am empty.

*

It smashed against the grating
and slipped down quickly out of sight.
It was over in a comical flash.
The soft mucous shell clung a little longer,
then drained down.

She stood staring, in blank anger.
Then her eyes came to life, and she laughed
and let the bird flap away.
'It's all the one.
There's plenty more where that came from!'

Hen to pan!
It was a simple world.

A HAND OF SOLO

Lips and tongue
wrestle the delicious
    life out of you.

A last drop.
Wonderful.
    A moment's rest.

In the firelight glow
the flickering
    shadows softly

come and go up on the shelf:
red heart and black spade
    hid in the kitchen dark.

Woman throat song
help my head
    back to you sweet.

*

Hushed, buried green baize.
Slide and stop. Black spades. Tray. Still.
Red deuce. Two hearts. Blood-clean. Still.

Black flash. Jack Rat grins.
She drops down. Silent. Face disk blank. Queen.

The Boss spat in the kitchen fire.
His head shook.

Angus's fat hand brushed in all the pennies.
His waistcoat pressed the table.

Uncle Matty slithered the cards together
and knocked them. Their edges melted. Soft gold.

Angus picked up a bright penny and put it
in my hand: satiny, dream-new disk of light . . .

'Go on out in the shop and get yourself something.'
'Now, Angus . . .'
                    'Now, now, Jack. He's my luck.'
'Tell your grandmother we're waiting for her.'

She was settling the lamp.
Two yellow tongues rose and brightened.
The shop brightened.

Her eyes glittered.
A tin ghost beamed, Mick McQuaid
nailed across the fireplace.

'Shut the kitchen door, child of grace.
Come here to me.
Come here to your old grandmother.'

Strings of jet beads wreathed her neck
and hissed on the black taffeta
and crept on my hair.

'. . . You'd think I had three heads!'
My eyes were squeezed shut against the key
in the pocket of her apron. Her stale abyss . . .

Old knuckles pressed on the counter,
then were snatched away. She sat down at the till
on her high stool, chewing nothing.

The box of Indian apples
was over in the corner
by the can of oil.

I picked out one of the fruit,
a rose-red hard wax
turning toward gold, light like wood,

and went at it with little bites,
peeling off bits of skin
and tasting the first traces of the blood.

When it was half peeled,
with the glassy pulp exposed like cells,
I sank my teeth in it

loosening the packed mass of dryish beads
from their indigo darkness.
I drove my tongue among them

and took a mouthful, and slowly
bolted them. My throat filled
with a rank, Arab bloodstain.

THE HIGH ROAD

Don't be too long now, the next time.
She hugged me tight in behind the counter.
Here! she whispered. (A silvery
little mandoline, out of the sweet-box.)

They were standing waiting in the sun outside
at the shop door, with the go car,
their long shadows along the path.

A horse trotted past us down Bow Lane;
Padno Carty sat in the trap
sideways, fat, drifting along
with a varnish twinkle of spokes and redgold
balls of manure scattering
on the road behind.
               Mrs. Fullerton
was sitting on a stool in her doorway,
beak-nosed, one eye dead.
DARK! DAAARK! squawked the sour parrot
in her room. (Sticking to his cage
with slow nails, upside down.
He mumbles on a bar, and creeps
stiffly, crossways, with his tongue;
a black moveable nut
               mumble
il my moulh.)
            Silvery tiny strings
trembled in my brain.
               Over the parapet of
the bridge at the end of Granny and Granda's
the brown water poured and gurgled

141

over the stones and tin cans in the Camac,
down by the back of Aunty Josie's.
A stony darkness, after the bridge,
trickled down Cromwell's Quarters, step
by step, along by the foot of the wall,
from James's Street.
                    (A mob of shadows
mill in silence on the Forty Steps;
horse-ghosts back and plunge, turning
under slow swords. In the Malt Stores,
through a barred window on one of the steps,
spectres huddle everywhere
among the shadowy brick pillars
and dunes of grain, watching
the pitch drain out of their wounds.)

Up the High Road I held hands,
inside on the path, beside the warm
feathery grass, and looked through the paling,
pulled downward by a queer feeling.
Down there . . . Small front gardens
getting lower and lower; doorways,
windows, below the road.
On the clay slope on the other side
a path slants up and disappears
into the Robbers' Den. I crept up
the last stretch to the big hole
full of fright, once, and knelt
on the clay to look inside:
it was only a hollow someone made,
with a dusty piece of man's dung
and a few papers in a corner,
and bluebottles.

        (Not even in my mind
has one silvery string picked
a single sound. And it will never.)

Above the far-off back yards
the breeze gave a sigh: a sin happening . . .
I let go and stopped, and looked down
at a space in the weeds, and let it fall
for ever into empty space
toward a stone shed, and saw it turn
over with a tiny flash,
silvery shivering with loss.

ANCESTOR

I was going up to say something,
and stopped. Her profile against the curtains
was old, and dark like a hunting bird's.

It was the way she perched on the high stool,
staring into herself, with one fist
gripping the side of the barrier around her desk
— or her head held by something, from inside.
And not caring for anything around her
or anyone there by the shelves.
I caught a faint smell, musky and queer.

I may have made some sound — she stopped rocking
and pressed her fist in her lap; then she stood up
and shut down the lid of the desk, and turned the key.
She shoved a small bottle under her aprons
and came toward me, darkening the passageway.

Ancestor . . .   among sweet- and fruit-boxes.
Her black heart . . .
                    Was that a sigh?
— brushing by me in the shadows,
with her heaped aprons, through the red hangings
to the scullery, and down to the back room.

TEAR

I was sent in to see her.
A fringe of jet drops
chattered at my ear
as I went in through the hangings.

I was swallowed in chambery dusk.
My heart shrank
at the smell of disused
organs and sour kidney.

The black aprons I used to
bury my face in
were folded at the foot of the bed
in the last watery light from the window

(Go in and say goodbye to her)
and I was carried off
to unfathomable depths.
I turned to look at her.

She stared at the ceiling
and puffed her cheek, distracted,
propped high in the bed
resting for the next attack.

The covers were gathered close
up to her mouth,
that the lines of ill-temper still
marked. Her grey hair

was loosened out like
a young woman's all over
the pillow, mixed with the shadows
criss-crossing her forehead

and at her mouth and eyes,
like a web of strands tying down her head
and tangling down toward the shadow
eating away the floor at my feet.

I couldn't stir at first, nor wished to,
for fear she might turn and tempt me
(my own father's mother)
with open mouth

— with some fierce wheedling whisper —
to hide myself one last time
against her, and bury my
self in her drying mud.

Was I to kiss her? As soon
kiss the damp that crept
in the flowered walls
of this pit.

Yet I had to kiss.
I knelt by the bulk of the death bed
and sank my face in the chill
and smell of her black aprons.

Snuff and musk, the folds against my eyelids,
carried me into a derelict place
smelling of ash: unseen walls and roofs
rustled like breathing.

I found myself disturbing
dead ashes for any trace
of warmth, when far off
in the vaults a single drop

splashed. And I found
what I was looking for
— not heat nor fire,
not any comfort,

but her voice, soft, talking to someone
about my father: 'God help him, he cried
big tears over there by the machine
for the poor little thing.' Bright

drops on the wooden lid for
my infant sister. My own
wail of child-animal grief
was soon done, with any early guess

at sad dullness and tedious pain
and lives bitter with hard bondage.
How I tasted it now —
her heart beating in my mouth!

She drew an uncertain breath
and pushed at the clothes
and shuddered tiredly.
I broke free

and left the room
promising myself
when she was really dead
I would really kiss.

My grandfather half looked up
from the fireplace as I came out,
and shrugged and turned back
with a deaf stare to the heat.

I fidgeted beside him for a minute
and went out to the shop.
It was still bright there
and I felt better able to breathe.

Old age can digest
anything: the commotion
at Heaven's gate — the struggle
in store for you all your life.

How long and hard it is
before you get to Heaven,
unless like little Agnes
you vanish with early tears.

IRWIN STREET

Morning sunlight — a patch of clear memory —
warmed the path and
the crumbling brick wall,
and stirred the weeds sprouting
in the mortar.
               A sparrow cowered
on a doorstep. Under the broken door
the paw of a cat reached out.
White nails fastened in the feathers.

Aware — a distinct dream —
as though slowly making it happen.
The suitcase in my hand.
                     My schoolbooks . . .

I turned the corner into the avenue
between the high wire fence and the trees
in the Hospital: under the leaves
the road was empty and fragrant
with little lances of light.
He was coming toward me — how
could he be there, at this hour? —
my maker, in a white jacket,
and with my face. Our steps
hesitated in awkward greeting.

                 *

Wakening again, upstairs,
to the same wooden sourness.

I sat up on the edge of the bed,
my hand in my pyjama trousers,
my bare feet on the bare boards.

a single drop

NUCHAL
(a fragment)

'. . . down among the roots like a half-
buried vase brimming
over with pure water,
a film of clear brilliancy
spilling down its sides
rippling with reflections
of the four corners of the garden.
Fish-spirits slip down shimmering
into the grass; the grass
welcomes them with a hiss
of movement and voices
— its own snake-spirits.

On the last of the grass,
dreaming on one outstretched arm,
the woman lies smiling in her sleep.
Her arm dips over the brink
with the fingers trailing ladylike
in the water
                    — the rivulet
simply wanders up to her,
making to go past out of the garden,
meets her fingers
— and four sunlit ripples
lengthen out from them;
the stream divides and subdivides
into four, moistening and softening
the first downward curve of the hill.

She has dreamed so long already
— it is monstrous . . .

                    four great rivers
creep across the plain
toward the four corners of
                    that vast domain:

Eastward, a quiet river feeds the soil
till the soft banks crumble, caked with oil.
A sudden shine, out of eternal spring:
a crop of gold, with many a precious thing
— bdellium, seeking the pearl in its own breast,
the flower-figured onyx, the amethyst . . .

Southward (it seems of melted gold) a stream
rolls toward the summer in a fiery gleam,
leaving a honey of fertility
to sweeten the salt marsh in some degree.

A third runs Westward in its deeper bed,
tigrish, through narrow gorges, winy red,
as though some heart toward which it ran (a vein)
drew it onward through that cruel terrain.

Lastly, a milk-white river, faring forth
in a slow flood, laughing to the North.

Four rivers reaching toward th'encircling sea,
that bitter river,
                    where every . . .'

ENDYMION

At first there was nothing. Then a closed space.
Such light as there was showed him sleeping.
I stole nearer and bent down; the light grew brighter,
and I saw it came from the interplay of our two beings.
It blazed in silence as I kissed his eyelids.
I straightened up and it faded, from his pallor
and the ruddy walls with their fleshy thickenings
— great raw wings, curled — a huge owlet-stare —
as a single drop echoed in the depths.

SURVIVOR

High near the heart of the mountain there is a cavern.
There, under pressure in the darkness,
as the walls protest and give dryly,
sometimes you can hear minute dust-falls.
But there is no danger.
The cavern is a perfect shell of force;
the torsions that brought this place forth
maintain it. It is spoken of, always,
in terms of mystery — our first home . . .
that there is a power holding this part of the mountain
subtly separate from the world, in firm hands;
that this cave escaped the Deluge;
that it will play some part on the Last Day.

Far back, a lost echoing
single drop:
the musk of glands
and bloody gates and alleys.

Claws sprang open
starred with pain.

*

Curled in self hate. Delicious.
   Head heavy. Arm too heavy.
What is it, to suffer:
   the dismal rock nourishes.
Draughts creep: shelter in them.
   Deep misery: it is a pleasure.
Soil the self,
   lie still.

Utter dread
   of moving
the lips
   to let out
the offence simmering
   weakly
as possible
   within.

Something crept in once.
Was that a dream?
A flame of cold that crept under the back
and under the head huddled close
into the knees and belly.
For what seemed a long year
a thin thread of some kind of sweetness
wailed far below
in the grey valley of the blood.
What is there to remember?

Long ago, abuse and terror . . .

O fair beginning . . .

landfall — an entire new world
floating on the ocean like a cloud
with a forest covering and clean empty shores.
We were coming from . . .   Distilled from the sunlight?
or the crests of foam?
                    From Paradise . . .
In the southern coast of the East . . . In terror
— we were all thieves. In search of a land without sin
that might go unpunished, and so prowling
the known world—the northern portion, toward the West

(thinking, places answering each other on earth
might answer in nature).
Late afternoon we came in sight
of promontories beautiful beyond description
and saw the crystal sea gather in savage currents
and dash itself against the cliffs.
By twilight everything was destroyed,
the only survivors a shoal of women
spilled onto the shingle, and one man
that soon — even as they lifted themselves up
and looked about them in the dusk —
they silently surrounded.
Paradise!
       No serpents.
No lions. No toads. No injurious rats
or dragons or scorpions. No noxious beasts.
Only the she-wolf . . .

Everyone falling sick, after a time.

Perpetual twilight . . . with most of the light dissolved
in the soil and rocks and the uneasy waves.
A last outpost into the gloom. Sometimes
an otherworldly music sounded in the wind.
A land of the dead.
         Above the landing place
the grass shivered in the thin shale
at the top of the path, waiting, never again disturbed.
There was a great rock in the sea, where we went down
— The Hag: squatting on the water,
her muzzle staring up at nothing.

A final struggle up rocks and heather,
heart and lungs aching,
and thin voices in the valley
faintly calling, and dissolving one
by one in the blood.

I must remember
and be able some time to explain.

*

There is nothing here for sustenance.
   Unbroken sleep were best.
Hair. Claws. Grey.
   Naked. Wretch. Wither.

AT THE CROSSROADS

A dog's
body zipped
open and
stiff in
the grass.

They used to leave hanged men here.

A night when the moon is full
and swims with evil through the trees,
if you walk from the silent stone bridge
to the first crossroads and stand there,
do you feel that sad disturbance under the branches?
Three times I have been halted there
and had to whisper 'O Christ protect'
and not known whether my care was for myself
or some other hungry spirit.
Once by a great whiplash without sound.
Once by an unfelt shock at my ribs
as a phantom dagger stuck shuddering in nothing.
Once by a torch flare crackling
suddenly unseen in my face.
Three times, always at that same corner.
Never altogether the same. But the same.

Once when I had worked like a dull ox
in patience to the point of foolishness
I found myself rooted here, my thoughts
scattered by the lash Clarity:
the end of labour is in sacrifice,
the beast of burden in his shuddering prime
— or in leaner times any willing dogsbody.

A white face
stared from the
void, tilted over,
her mouth ready.

And all mouths everywhere so
in their need, turning on each furious
other. Flux of forms
in a great stomach: living meat torn off,
enduring in one mess of terror
every pang it sent through every thing
it ever, in shudders of pleasure, tore.

A white ghost flickered into being
and disappeared near the tree tops.
An owl in silent scrutiny
with blackness in her heart. She
who succeeds from afar . . .

                    The choice —
the drop with deadened wing-beats; some creature
torn and swallowed; her brain, afterward,
staring among the rafters in the dark
until hunger returns.

SACRIFICE

Crowded steps, a sea of white faces
streaked with toil.

The scrutiny is over, in sunlight,
terrible black and white.

There is the mark . . .   In those streaks . . .
Their hands are on her.
Her friends gather.
The multitudes sigh and bless
and persuade her heavily forward to her tears
in doomed excitement
down the cup of light
and onto her back on the washed bricks
with breasts held apart
and midriff fluttering in the sun.

The souls gather unseen, like wisps of hunger,
hovering above the table, not interfering,
as it is done in a shivering flash.
The vivid pale solid of the breast
dissolves in a crimson flood.
The heart flops in its sty.

*

Never mind the hurt. I've never felt
so terribly alive, so ready, so gripped
by love — gloved fingers slippery
next the heart!
                    Is it very difficult?

The blinding pain — when love goes direct
and wrenches at the heart-strings! But the pangs
quickly pass their maximum, and then
such a fount of tenderness!

                                      Are you stuck?
Let me arch back.

                        I love how you keep muttering
'You know now . . .' — and your concern . . .
but you must finish it.
I lose my mind gladly, thinking:
the heart — in another's clutches!

We are each other's knowledge. It is peace that counts,
and knowledge brings peace, even thrust crackling
into the skull and bursting with tongues of fire.
Peace. Love dying down, as love ascends.

I love your tender triumph, straightening up,
lifting your reddened sleeves. The stain spreads downward
through your great flushed pinions.
You are a real angel.
My heart is in your hands: mind it well.

nightnothing

ALL IS EMPTINESS,
AND I MUST SPIN

A vacancy in which, apparently
I hang
      with severed senses

         *

I have been in places . . .

The floors crept,
an electric terror
waited everywhere
— just one touch!

We were made to separate
and strip. My urine flowed
with mild excitement.
Our hands touched lightly
in farewell.

Permit me, with drunken pleasure . . .

         *

How bring oneself to judge, or think,
so hurled onward!
            inward!

After a while, in the utter darkness,
there was a slight but perceptible
movement of the air.
It was not Death, but Night . . .

mountain coolness; a tiny
freshness of dew on the face
— tears of self forming.

I was lying in utter darkness
in a vaulted place. Cold air
crept over long-abandoned floors,
bearing a taint of remote iron
and dead ash: the interior
of some extinct . . .
                    A distant door
clangs. Echo of voices.

                    *

The sterile: it is a whole matter in itself.
Fantastic millions of
fragile

in every single

ELY PLACE

Sunday.
       'Such a depth of charm
here always . . .'
           Doomed in the sun.
In Mortuary Lane a gull
cried on one of the Hospital gutters
— I. I. I . . . harsh
in sadness, on and on,
beak and gullet open
against the blue.
         Down at the corner
a flicker of sex, a white
dress, against the railings.

'This is where George Moore . . .'
              rasps

his phantom walking-stick
without a sound, toward the Post Office
where her slight body, in white,
has disappeared.
       (A flustered
perfumy dress — a mothering
shocked smile — live muscle
startling in skin.)

       A blood vision
started out of the brick: the box
of keys in my pocket — I am opening it,
tongue-tied. I unpick the little
pen-knife and dig it in her throat,
her spirting gullet!
        Vanishing . . .

Indoors, darkness pours down
through half light stale as the grave
over plates and silver bowls
glimmering on a side table.
Vanishing . . .

                Solid matter
flickering in broad daylight

(and they are on it in a flash,
brief tongues of movement
ravenous, burrowing and feeding,
invisible in blind savagery,
upstreaming through the sunlight with it
until it disappears, buried
in heaven, faint, far off).

' . . . with a wicked wit, but self-mocking;
and full of integrity behind it all . . .'

A few beginnings, a few
tentative tired endings over
and over . . .

                Memoirs, maggots.

                      After lunch
a quarter of an hour at most ·
of empty understanding.

TOUCHING THE RIVER

That nude kneeling so sad-seeming
on her shelf of moss, how timelessly
— all sepia — her arm reaches down
to let her fingers, affectedly trailing,
stick in the stopped brown water.

Rivery movement; gurgling, clay-fresh;
light murmuring over the surface;
bubbling . . .
                Our unstopped
flesh and senses — how they vanish!

Though we kneel on the brink and drive our stare
down — *now* — into the current.
Though everywhere in the wet fields — listen —
the reeds are shivering (one clump of them
nestling a lark's eggs, I know, in a hoof-print).

THE LIFFEY HILL

The path climbs up to the left, toward the **Plantation**
(tree trunks, a clay floor, dim and still,
papers and bottles scattered everywhere
and lodging in the roots), then to the right
across the grass slope.
                              It opens onto the top,
a long field narrowing down
in bushes and wire at the far end

where the snow hushed
on Christmas morning
and we followed the rabbit tracks
dotted along light and powdery everywhere
and found the white silence
under a stillness of twigs
breathless with carefulness
where the rabbit went
                              where?
whirring past
              a bird

Snow powdery pure
on the wool glove, detailed and soft.
The day lengthened, and the wool got dark and wet
and smelled of cold.
                    Flatsour? Raw . . . notsour

Morning, the magical-bright first print, gone . . .
The air grew dark, and harder.
We are out too late.
Voices, far away, die in the cold.

But there is still the pleasure of going home,
and dusk closing in, and a good fire.

I scrambled on top of the wall in the lamp-light,
bundled up in scarf and coat,
and hugged the iron post, and slipped down.
My boots scuffled on the path,
echoing, alone,
                down the Lane.

GOOD NIGHT

It is so peaceful, at last:
the heat creeping through the house,
the floorboards reacting in the corner.
The voices in the next room
boom on in their cabinet.
How it brings out the least falseness!
There is one of them chuckling at
a quiet witticism of his own.

Relax, and these things
shall be . . .
           and the voices of a norm
that is in course of . . .
                foundering . . .
urgent yet mannerly:
I would remind . . . Please . . .
Oblivion, our natural condition . . .

and the sounds of the house are all
flowing into one another and turning
in one soft-booming, slowly swallowing
vertige most soothing and pleasant
down this suddenly live
brinegullet
            to a drowned pit
clasping the astonished spectre of
the psyche in its sweet wet.

Attached into the darkness by every sense
— the ear pounding —
peering eye-apples, unseeing —

171

fingers and tongue
                    outstretched —
into a nothingness
inhabited by a vague animal light
from the walls and floor.
Out of the glassy rock,
like tentacles moving on each other
near their soft roots, human thighs
are growing; if you look closely
you can see the tender undermost
muscle actually forming
from the rock, and the living veins
continuing inward, just visible
under the skin, and (faintly lit from within)
clusters of soft arms gathering down
tiny open eyes, finger-tips, pursed
mouths from the gloom, minute
drifting corruscations of light, glistening
little gnat-crescents of hair!

What essences, disturbed from what
profounder nothingness . . .
flickering, delicate
and distinct, fondled
blindly and drawn down
into what sense or languor

. . . Would you agree, then, we won't
find truths, or any certainties . . .

where monsters lift soft
self-conscious voices, and feed us
and feed in us, and coil
and uncoil in our substance,

so that in that they are there
we cannot know them, and that,
daylit, we are the monsters of our night,
and somewhere the monsters of our night are . . .
here . . . in daylight that our nightnothing
feeds in and feeds, wandering
out of the cavern, a low cry
echoing — Camacamacamac . . .

that we need as we don't need truth . . .

and ungulfs a Good Night, smiling.

OTHER POEMS

THE ROUTE OF THE TAIN

Gene sat on a rock, dangling our map.
The others were gone over the next crest,
further astray. We ourselves, irritated,
were beginning to turn down toward the river
back to the car, the way we should have come.

We should have trusted our book —
after they tried a crossing, and this river too
'rose against them' and bore off
a hundred of their charioteers toward the sea
They had to move along the river Colptha
up to its source
     there:
where the main branch sharpens away gloomily
to a gash in the hill opposite;
then to Bélat Ailiúin
       by that pathway
climbing back and forth out of the valley
over to Ravensdale.

Scattering in irritation . . . who had set out
so cheerfully to celebrate our book;
cheerfully as we made and remade it
through a waste of hours, content to 'enrich the present
honouring the past', each to his own just function . . .
Wandering off, ill-sorted,
like any beasts of the field,
one snout honking disconsolate,
another burrowing in its pleasures . . .

When not far above us a red fox
ran at full stretch out of the bracken
and panted across the hillside toward the next ridge.

Where he vanished — a faint savage sharpness
out of the earth — an inlet of the sea
shone in the distance at the mouth of the valley
beyond Omeath: grey waters crawled with light.

For a heartbeat, in alien certainty,
we exchanged looks. We should have known it, by now:
the process, the whole tedious
enabling ritual! Flux brought to fullness
— saturated — the clouding over — dissatisfaction
spreading slowly like an ache: something
reduced shivering suddenly into meaning
along new boundaries
                        — through a forest,
by a salt-dark shore,
by a standing stone on a dark plain,
by a ford running blood,
and along this gloomy pass, with someone ahead
calling and waving on the crest, against a heaven
of dismantling cloud — transfixed
by the same figure (stopped, pointing)
on the rampart at Cruachan
where it began . . .
the morning sunlight pouring on us all
as we scattered over the mounds
disputing over useless old books,
assembled in cheerful speculation
around a prone block, *Miosgán Medba,*
— Queen Medb's *turd* . . . ? — and rattled our maps,
joking together in growing illness
or age or fat; before us
the route of the Táin, over men's dust,
toward these hills that seemed to grow
darker as we drove nearer.

WORKER IN MIRROR, AT HIS BENCH

I
Silent rapt surfaces
assemble glittering
among themselves.

A few more pieces.

What to call it . . .
                              Bright Assembly?
Foundations for a Tower?
Open Trap? Circular-Tending
Self-Reflecting Abstraction . . .

II
The shop doorbell rings.
A few people enter.

I'm sorry, I'm afraid you've caught me
a little early in my preparations.
Forgive me
                    — the way they mess
with everything —
                              I am an indolent sinner.

Smile. How they tighten their lips:
What *is* it about the man
that is so impossible to like?
The flashy coat, the flourished cuffs?
The ease under questioning . . .

Yes, everything is deliberate.

This floppy flower. Smile.
This old cutaway style
— all the easier to bare the breast.
Comfortable smiles.
               A cheap lapse —
forgive me: the temptation never sleeps.
The smiles more watery.

No, it has no practical application.
I am simply trying to understand something
— states of peace nursed out of wreckage.
The peace of fullness, not emptiness.

It is tedious, yes.
The process is elaborate, and wasteful
— a dangerous litter of lacerating pieces
collects. Let my rubbish stand witness . . .
Smile, stirring it idly with a shoe.
Take, for example, this work in hand:
out of its waste matter
it should emerge light and solid.
One idea, grown with the thing itself,
should drive it searching inward
with a sort of life, due to the mirror effect.
Often, the more I simplify,
the more a few simplicities go
burrowing into their own depths,
until the guardian structure is aroused . . .

Most satisfying, yes.
Another kind of vigour, I agree
— unhappy until its actions are more convulsed:
the 'passionate' — might find it maddening.

Here the passion is in the putting together.

Yes, I suppose I am appalled
at the massiveness of others' work.
But not deterred; I have leaned my shed
against a solid wall. Understanding smiles.
I tinker with the things that dominate me
as they describe their random
persistent coherences . . .
clean surfaces shift
and glitter among themselves . . .

Pause. We all are vile . . .
Let the voice die away.

Awkward silence.
They make their way out.

But they are right to be suspicious
when answers distract and conceal.
What is there to understand?
Time punishes — and this
the flesh teaches. Emptiness,
is that not peace?

Conceal, and permit . . .
— pursuit at its most delicate,
truth as tinkering,
easing the particular of its litter,
bending attention on the remaining depths
as though questions had never been . . .

III

He bends closer, testing the work.
The bright assembly begins to turn in silence.
The answering brain glitters — one system
answering another. The senses enter
and reach out with a pulse of pleasure
to the four corners of their own wilderness:

a gold mask, vast
in the distance, stares back.
Familiar features.
Naked sky-blue eyes
(It is morning
once upon a time.)
Disappears.
Was it a dream?
Forgotten.

Reappears: enormous
and wavering. Silver.
Stern and beautiful,
with something not yet pain in the eyes.
The forehead begins to wrinkle:
what ancient sweet time . . .
Forgotten.

Re-establishes:
a bronze head thrown back
across the firmament,
a bronze arm covering the eyes.
Pain established.
Eyes that have seen . . .
Forgotten.

Dark as iron.
All the light hammered
into two blazing eyes;
all the darkness
into one wolf-muzzle.
Resist!
An unholy tongue laps, tastes
brothers' thick blood.
Forget!

He straightens up, unseeing.

Did I dream another outline
in the silt of the sea floor?
Blunt stump of limb —
a marble carcase
where no living thing can have crept,
below the last darkness,
slowly, as the earth ages,
blurring with pressure.
The calm smile of a half-
buried face: eyeball
blank, the stare inward
to the four corners of
what foul continuum . . .

blackness — all matter
in one light-devouring
polished cliff-face
hurtling rigid
from zenith to pit
through dead

DROWSING OVER THE ARABIAN NIGHTS

I nodded. The books agree,
one hopes for too much.
It is ridiculous.
We are elaborate beasts.

If we concur it is only
in our hunger — the soiled gullet . . .
and sleep's airy nothing;
and the moist matter of lust

(if the whole waste of women
could be gathered like one pit
under swarming Man . . .
— then all might act together!);

and the agonies of death,
as we enter our endless nights
quickly, one by one, fire
darting up to the roots of our hair.

THE CLEARING

'. . . there is so little I can do any more
but it is nearly done . . .'

It is night. A troubled figure
is moving about its business
muttering between the fire and the gloom.
Impenetrable growth surrounds him.
Owlful. Batful.
Great moths of prey.

'. . . and still the brainworm will not sleep
squirming behind the eyes
staring out from its narrow box . . .'

He stops suddenly and straightens.
The eyes grow sharper
— and the teeth!

'. . . and then the great ease
when something that was stalking us
is taken — the head cut off
held by the fur
the blood dropping hot
the eye-muscles star-bright to my jaws! . . '

ST. PAUL'S ROCKS: 16 FEBRUARY 1832

A cluster of rocks far from the trade routes
a thousand miles from any other land
they appear abruptly in the ocean,
low lying, so hidden in driving mists
they are seldom sighted, and then briefly,
white and glittering against the eternal grey.

Despite the lack of any vegetation
they have succeeded in establishing
symbiosis with the surrounding water.
Colonies of birds eat the abundant fish;
moths feed on the feathers; lice and beetles
live in the dung; countless spiders
prey on these scavangers; in the crevices
a race of crabs lives on the eggs and young.

In squalor and killing and parasitic things
life takes its first hold.
Later the noble accident: the seed, dropped
in some exhausted excrement, or bobbing
like a matted skull into an inlet.

THE DISPOSSESSED

The lake is deserted now
but the water is still clean and transparent,
the headlands covered with laurels,
the little estuaries full of shells,
with enchanting parterres where the waves
ebb and flow over masses of turf and flowers.

It was like a miracle, a long pastoral, long ago.
The intoxication of a life gliding away
in the face of heaven: Spring, a plain of flowers;
Autumn, with grape-clusters and chestnuts
formed in its depths; our warm nights
passing under starlight.
                     We had established peace,
having learnt to practise virtue without
expectation of recompense — that we must be virtuous
without hope. (The Law is just; observe it,
maintain it, and it will bring contentment.)

Then, by the waterside, among the tortoises
with their mild and lively eyes, with crested larks
fluttering around Him, so light
they rested on a blade of grass
without bending it, He came among us
and lifted His unmangled hand:
                        These beauties,
these earth-flowers growing and blowing, what are they?
The spectacle of your humiliation!
If a man choose to enter the kingdom of peace
he shall not cease from struggle until he fail,
and having failed he will be astonished,
and having been astonished will rule,

and having ruled will rest.

                                    Our dream curdled.
We awoke, and began to thirst
for the restoration of our house.
One morning, in a slow paroxysm of rage,
we found His corpse stretched on the threshold.

DEATH BED

Motionless — his sons —
we watched his brows draw together with strain.
The wind tore at the leather walls of our tent;
two grease lamps fluttered
at the head and foot of the bed.
Our shadows sprang here and there.

At that moment our sign might
have coursed across the heavens,
and we had spared no one to watch.

*

Our people are most vulnerable to loss
when we gather like this to one side,
around some death,

and try to weave it into our lives
— who can weave nothing but our ragged
routes across the desert.

And it is those among us
who most make the heavens their business
who go most deeply into this death-weaving.

As if the star might
spring from the dying mouth
or shoot from the agony of the eyes.

'We must not miss it,
however it comes.'
— If it comes.

*

He stretched out his feet
and seemed to sink deeper in the bed,
and was still.
                    Sons no longer,
we pulled down his eyelids
and pushed the chin up gently to close his mouth,
and stood under the flapping roof.
Our shelter sheltered under the night.

                    *

Hides, furs and skins,
are our shelter and our garments.

We can weave nothing.

CRAB ORCHARD SANCTUARY: LATE OCTOBER

The lake water lifted a little and fell
doped and dreamy in the late heat.
The air at lung temperature — like the end of the world:
a butterfly panted with dull scarlet wings
on the mud by the reeds, the tracks
of small animals softening along the edge,
a child's foot-prints, out too far . . .

The car park was empty. Long threads of spider silk
blew out softly from the tips of the trees.
A big spider stopped on the warm gravel,
sunlight charging the dark shell.

A naked Indian stepped out onto the grass
silent and savage, faded,
grew transparent, disappeared.

A speedboat glistened slowly in the distance.
A column of smoke climbed from the opposite shore.
In the far inlets clouds of geese flew about
quarreling and settling in.

*

        That morning
two thin quails appeared in our garden
stepping one by one with piping movements
across the grass, feeding. I watched a long time
until they rounded the corner of the house.
A few grey wasps still floated about at the eaves;
crickets still chirruped in the grass

— but in growing silence — after last week's frosts.
Now a few vacated bodies, locust wraiths,
light as dry scale, begin to drift
on the driveway among the leaves,
stiff little Fuseli devil bodies.
Hidden everywhere, a myriad
leather seed-cases lie in wait
nourishing curled worms of white fat
— ugly, in absolute certainty, piteous,
threatening in every rustling sound:
bushes worrying in the night breeze,
dry leaves detaching, and creeping.
They will swarm again, on suffocated nights,
with their endless hysterics; and wither away again.

*

Who will stand still then, listening
to that woodpecker knocking, and watch
the erratic jays and cardinals flashing
blue and red among the branches and trunks;
that bronze phantom pausing; and this . . . stock-still,
with glittering brain, withering away.

It is an ending already.
The road hot and empty, taken over
by spiders, and pairs of butterflies twirling
about one another, and grasshoppers leap-
drifting over the gravel, birds darting
fluttering through the heat.
                              What solitary step.

A slow hot glare out on the lake
spreading over the water.

WYNCOTE, PENNSYLVANIA: A GLOSS

A mocking-bird on a branch
outside the window, where I write,
gulps down a wet crimson berry,
shakes off a few bright drops
from his wing, and is gone
into a thundery sky.

Another storm coming.
Under that copper light
my papers seem luminous.
And over them I will take
ever more painstaking care.